the CHRISTMAS COOKIE book

ALMOND TILES

the CHRISTMAS COOKIE book

BY **lou seibert pappas**

PHOTOGRAPHS BY **frankie frankeny**

CHRONICLE BOOKS
SAN FRANCISCO

ACKNOWLEDGMENTS

For sharing their prized Christmas cookies,
many thanks to special friends:
Tina Dreyer, Ruby Lomax, Diane Reuland,
Corinna Shirk, Marge Sternlieb,
Jane Stocklin, and Phyllis Silverstein.

Library of Congress Cataloging-in-Publication Data available

ISBN: 0-8118-3095-0

Printed in Hong Kong

Book Design: Anne Galperin
Food Stylist: Diane Gsell
Photo Assistant: Lissa Ivy Tiegel
Prop Styling: Carol Hacker, Monica Heinemann, JoAnn Frankeny
Package Design: Alyson Kuhn

Distributed in Canada by Raincoast Books
9050 Shaughnessy Street
Vancouver, British Columbia V6P 6E5

10 9 8 7 6

Chronicle Books LLC
85 Second Street
San Francisco, California 94105

www.chroniclebooks.com

❧ CONTENTS ❧

❧ INTRODUCTION ❧

As a child, I remember metal tins jammed full of cookies year-around. There were inevitably two or three different kinds on the countertop, ready for grabbing by eager hands in search of an after-school snack or something extra for a brown-bag lunch. But come Christmastime, the kitchen was abuzz with baking activity nearly continuously, and the variety of cookies multiplied dramatically. Mother manned the big commercial Hobart mixer, turning out countless doughs particular to the holiday season, and we children joined in for the cutting and decorating.

Squirting out the *spritz* dough was a ritual everyone enjoyed. Mother treasured this Swedish butter confection of her forebears, as her aunt had owned a bakery in Gothenburg at the turn of the twentieth century. We made trees and stars out of sugar-cookie dough and dressed them up with colored sugars, and fashioned a favorite holiday confection out of husky Brazil nuts and sweet dried fruits. The doorbell rang and our neighbors presented us with tantalizing plate-fuls of *Springerle*, *Lebkuchen*, Scotch shortbread, and Mexican wedding cakes—new temptations to which I easily succumbed.

Later, on trips to Europe and elsewhere, I was greeted by a wealth of brand-new Christmas cookies. Marzipan and praline were tantalizing discoveries, especially the Scandinavian golden almond confections shaped like teardrops and dripping with frosting icicles. An eye-catching chocolate drop sealed in chocolate snow and showered with pistachios was irresistible in Helsinki. The spicy candied ginger cookies hawked along the canals in Amsterdam soon became addictive.

Visits to German Christmas markets introduced me to the endless variations of *Lebkuchen* and the decorative *Springerle*. Museum tours showed off the beautiful wooden molds and offered the history of their making, as I pursued the land—and cookie jar—of half my roots.

In Vienna I would duck into coffeehouses for a luscious chocolate-sealed marzipan wafer or a vanilla crescent to munch along with my *Kaffee mit Schlag.* In the French countryside, wafer-thin almond tiles reigned on the platefuls of *mignardises* offered with coffee. Hazelnuts starred in Switzerland, where the chocolate-sealed spice wafers were divine. In Italy, I was drawn to sophisticated Florentines and nut macaroons, and on a trip to Australia, I discovered a nine-inch-long macadamia-ginger twice-baked cookie.

Back home, I married into a Greek family and was quickly captivated by my in-laws' sugar-dusted *kourabiedes.* As my four children grew up, these traditional cookies became a must-do Christmastime treat. Over the years, my cookie repertoire has continued to expand, and each December more tins in all shapes and sizes are filled with time-honored holiday favorites.

Christmas is a time for extra-special cookies—baked with children, festively wrapped for gift giving, boxed for mailing, and served at parties. They are a joyous way to share the spirit of the season with family, neighbors, and friends. This collection of delectable Christmas cookies, divided into four chapters, fits all those holiday roles.

The first recipe chapter, **TIMELESS TRADITIONAL COOKIES**, includes nearly a dozen holiday classics, many of which have been baked for centuries. Over time they have been refined and perfected, and Christmas in Germany, Sweden, or elsewhere simply wouldn't be the same without them.

In the second chapter, **FAMILY FAVORITES**, two complementary types of recipes are joined. The first are those that are a joy for children and teenagers to cut, bake, and decorate. The remaining recipes are family favorites—my family and friends' families—that have become an indispensable part of the holiday season, often because of their use of seasonal fruits, such as persimmons and cranberries, but also because of generations of tradition.

Everyone loves to receive a batch of cookies, and the third chapter, **COOKIES FOR GIFT GIVING & MAILING**, is divided into special cookies to wrap and hand-deliver and sturdier, packable cookies to box and ship by overnight or two-day service. The gift cookies for sharing with nearby friends and neighbors are often quite decorative, ideal for wrapping in a festive way. Sometimes a see-through container is appropriate, or perhaps a rattan basket festooned with red and green ribbons. Cookies suitable for mailing, a quality noted in the recipe introductions, are those that stand up well to travel and don't show their age.

The final chapter, **ELEGANT PARTY COOKIES**, is a showcase of gems that you will want to make when your family and friends join you for a holiday celebration. These can be the more fragile cookies, as they need only go from tin to table, and many of them can be baked and frozen in advance, to ease last-minute pressures on the always-busy party host.

Now, armed with this recipe box packed with holiday cookies, you can make every Christmas season a time filled with irresistible sweets shared with family and friends.

A SHORT HISTORY OF CHRISTMAS COOKIES

Since medieval times, Christmas cookies have been a tradition in northern and central Europe, particularly Scandinavia, Holland, and Germany. Many of these cookies are formed by using carved wooden molds to stamp out fruits, animals, human figures, or hearts.

German *Lebkuchen,* honey spice cookies that are the ancestor of gingerbread, are typically made in the shape of a heart or of Saint Nicholas. They are sold today in German villages at street fairs and in big city markets from the beginning of Advent until Christmas. Germany's anise-scented *Springerle* date back to midwinter festivals at which animals were sacrificed to the gods, but because the poor could not afford to butcher their animals, they offered baked tokens in the form of animal cookies. Many of these offerings took the shape of a rearing steed, as the word *Springerle* derives from the German phrase for "a vaulting horse." Town bakers were frequently responsible for the beautiful early molds that we now see in museums. The shop with the prettiest cookies was likely to capture the biggest holiday trade.

Until the Middle Ages, adding spices to cookie dough was uncommon, however. Spices were rare and costly, affordable only by the wealthy, a situation that prompted bakers to use ginger and pepper interchangeably. This fact explains why so many Christmastime and year-round ginger cookies have a pepper prefix, even though they lack that spice as an ingredient. Swedish *pepparkakor* and German *Pfeffernüsse* are examples.

In Holland, the early molds for *speculaas,* a spice cookie, depicted holiday scenes or events. These popular cookies were also favored as a way of delivering announcements or messages, by stamping words into the cookies before they were slipped into the oven.

Farther north, in Scotland, shortbread has long been a traditional Christmas and New Year's treat. The rich butter cake descends from the oatmeal bannock served at pagan Yule celebrations. The round bannock was scored in the center with a circle surrounded by wedges. This was meant to symbolize the sun and its rays. Because it was considered unlucky to cut the shortbread into portions, it was always broken into pieces by hand.

For centuries, *spritz* cookies, beloved in Sweden and Denmark, have been extruded from cookie presses into rounds, wreaths, and S's. Emigrants from these countries quickly popularized the buttery cookies when they settled in new homes in America.

Some version of peppernuts, spicy morsels the size of a nut, can be found in a handful of European countries. In Holland they are *pepernoten,* in Denmark *pebernodder,* and in Germany *Pfeffernüsse.* Creating them was a community affair: the dough was mixed and left to mellow in crocks for months, then rolled out assembly-line fashion, baked, and stored in jars until Christmas, when they would be eaten.

In Italy, cookies have mainly been the domain of the *pasticcerie,* or pastry shops, and home cooks simply bought their cookies. The almond paste cookies that are favorites throughout the country probably stem from the marzipan of Sicily that arrived with the Arabs. They also introduced cane sugar, almonds, and spices to the island. Nuns in the local convents perfected the recipes, adorning the cookies with angels and fondant frostings that resembled cathedral ceilings, and kept how to make them secret. In France as well, cookies were—and continue to be—the provenance of the professional baker, and the French traditionally visit their favorite pastry shops at holiday time, stocking up on delicate buttery cookies carefully packed in ribbon-bound boxes.

Today during the holiday season, families in many cultures bake and pass along their treasured family Christmas cookies, looking upon them as cherished heirlooms from past generations. This practice of sharing festive sweets made from traditional recipes is a wonderful way to renew old friendships and launch new ones.

THE BASICS

INGREDIENTS

High-quality ingredients are essential to turning out batches of the best cookies possible. To ensure that every cookie you bake has the finest flavor, always store ingredients properly and never use ingredients that are past their prime. The following annotated list includes pantry staples used in this book.

baking powder and baking soda

Baking powder and baking soda are both leavening agents, but they cannot be used interchangeably. Baking soda is only used in dough that contains an acid, such as brown sugar, yogurt, lemon juice, or molasses, to activate it. Baking powder must be stored airtight in a cool, dark place and used within 6 months, as it easily loses its leavening power. Stale baking powder may also leave an unpleasant aftertaste. Baking soda is not as perishable, but you should still update your supply once a year.

butter

Unsalted butter is preferred for making cookies, as it has a more delicate, fresher flavor than salted butter. A package labeled with the term *sweet cream butter* is misleading, as this is actually salted butter. The recipes were tested with unsalted butter, so if you use salted butter, you may want to reduce the salt called for in a recipe. While unsalted butter has a shorter refrigerator shelf life than salted butter, it keeps well in the freezer for up to 6 months.

chocolate and unsweetened cocoa powder

Chocolate products vary in amounts of sugar, cocoa butter, and chocolate liquor. Bittersweet and semisweet chocolate are similar, as both are sweetened, but bittersweet, which generally contains more chocolate liquor, often imparts a smoother, richer flavor. It is also usually less sweet than semisweet. Sometimes the two are interchangeable. Unsweetened chocolate is chocolate liquor and cocoa butter and it tastes quite bitter. Always purchase high-quality domestic or imported chocolate for the best baking results.

Unsweetened cocoa powder is made from the hardened cocoa liquor that remains after the making of chocolate. This solid mass is dried and ground to produce the powder. The richer Dutch-process cocoa powder has been treated to neutralize the natural acidity of cocoa.

eggs

All the recipes were tested with large eggs. If a recipe calls for separating the yolks and whites, make certain that the whites contain no egg yolk, as even a trace of yolk contains fat that prevents proper beating. If uncooked egg whites are specified in an icing and egg safety is a concern, use pasteurized egg whites.

flours

All-purpose flour, either bleached or unbleached, can be used in these recipes. This is a fine-textured flour that contains neither the germ nor the bran. Whole-wheat flour, which contains the wheat germ and natural bran of the grain, adds a fuller flavor and higher fiber content.

Nut flours, including almond, hazelnut (filbert), pecan, walnut, and pistachio, lend a wonderful flavor to many doughs.

nuts

Fresh top-quality nuts are essential. Refrigerate nuts for up to 2 months, or if you don't intend to use them within a short time, freeze them for up to 1 year. Longer storage results in diminished flavor. When a recipe calls for grinding nuts, it is smart to add a tablespoon of sugar to prevent the nuts from becoming an oily paste.

Toasting nuts helps bring out their flavor. Hazelnuts (filberts), however, are toasted not only to intensify their flavor, but also to remove their skins. Instructions for toasting all nuts are given below, under **MAKING & STORING COOKIES**. Sometimes one nut can be substituted for another. Use your own judgment, taking into consideration similar textures. Almonds and hazelnuts or walnuts and pecans are often interchangeable. With their green color, pistachios add a holiday look and can often substitute for walnuts.

Almond paste is a dense, stiff mixture of ground blanched almonds, sugar, and a syrupy liquid. It is available in 6- to 8-ounce cans and packages.

spices and flavorings

Purchase spices in stores that have a good turnover in stock, and store the spices in airtight containers in a cool pantry. Spices deteriorate in flavor after a year and can develop a musty flavor, so if you have kept them too long, discard them and buy a new supply. When vanilla or almond extract is called for, use a pure extract rather than an imitation or artificial one.

sweeteners

When simply *sugar* is specified in a recipe, use granulated sugar. Brown sugar comes in both light and dark styles, the dark being slightly stronger in flavor because it contains a bit more molasses. The brown sugars generally can be used interchangeably and should nearly always be firmly packed for the correct measure. If your brown sugar hardens, place a slice of apple in the container and it should soften within a day.

Powdered sugar, also known as confectioners' sugar, is granulated sugar that has been crushed to a fine powder. To prevent caking, it is mixed with about 3 percent cornstarch. Unless a recipe specifies sifting, it is not necessary to sift powdered sugar before using it. One cup of granulated sugar is equivalent to $1\frac{3}{4}$ cups (packed) powdered sugar.

Natural, unrefined, or milled brown sugars include honey-colored and large-grained demerara and turbinado, as well as the fine-grained, richly flavored light and dark muscovados, which are suitable for baking. These latter come from the island of Mauritius, off the coast of Africa, and only recently have become available in the United States.

Also in the marketplace are eye-catching decorating sugars in a broad spectrum of colors. Shapes vary from rounds to confetti to stamped-out designs. Some are sparkling. They are ideal for giving a Christmas spin to baked goods. Sources are listed on page 93.

Honey provides a fragrance and flavor depending on the flower nectar the bees visited. In general, the darker the color, the stronger the flavor. Orange blossom, clover, and sage are popular mild honeys.

Molasses, which comes in light and dark forms and is a by-product of sugar making, adds a robust flavor and rich color to baked goods. Unsulfured molasses, produced when no sulfur is used in the refining process, is preferred for its flavor, as sulfured molasses often carries a light sulfur taste.

EQUIPMENT

It is wise not to scrimp when you are shopping for equipment. Good equipment makes baking cookies easier, more enjoyable, and more successful. Nothing too fancy is needed, but everything you use should be top-notch. If you do not already have a cookie press or cookie molds, consider purchasing them for your holiday baking.

baking sheets

Well-made, clean baking sheets are essential to cookie success. Medium-weight aluminum sheets with just one or two narrow rims work well. (The absence of rims on two or three sides makes removing cookies easier.) Sheets that are dark or have blackened undersides disrupt the normal browning process. Nonstick cushioned sheets with a medium-light gray, rather than black, surface work well. It is useful to have at least two baking sheets.

measuring cups and spoons

Be sure to use the proper cups for measuring dry and wet ingredients. Cups for dry measures usually come in a graduated set from $\frac{1}{4}$ cup to 1 cup (sometimes $\frac{1}{8}$ cup is included), are made out of stainless steel or sturdy plastic, and have an even rim. Cups for liquid measures are typically clear glass or plastic, have vertical markings for fluid ounces and cups on the side, and include a pour spout. A set of measuring spoons, which are suitable for wet and dry measures, is also needed.

electric mixer

Most cookie doughs may be mixed by hand, but a handheld electric mixer is a great aid, especially for crumbly crusts for bar cookies, and an electric stand mixer is needed for doughs that require a wire whip for mixing.

food processor and blender

Some shortbread-type doughs and bar-cookie crusts work best if prepared in a food processor or with an electric mixer, due to the need for a crumbly consistency. Nuts and chocolate may be chopped by hand, but a blender or a food processor is handy for grinding them finely. It is a good idea to add 1 tablespoon of sugar to nuts when grinding them to prevent overprocessing, which results in an oily paste.

pastry bag

Although not necessary, a pastry bag is nice to have for adding icing decorations to cookies. Choose one with a variety of tips for the maximum versatility.

rack

A wire rack for cooling lets air circulate, so that the cookies cool evenly. Have a few in your cupboard for handling big cookie batches.

spatulas and cookie cutters

A thin-bladed, flexible spatula is essential for transferring cookies. A small icing spatula is ideal for decorating freshly baked cookies. A rubber spatula or plastic pastry scraper is useful for scraping dough from a bowl, while a rubber spatula is also ideal for doughs that require the folding in of ingredients and for cleaning down the sides of a blender or food processor. Cutters may be of any design or holiday motif you choose. Metal cutters give the best edge.

MAKING & STORING COOKIES

A handful of basic tips will make your cookie baking go smoothly and ensure that your stored batches stay deliciously fresh.

before you begin

Read the recipe *all the way through* before you take a mixing bowl or measuring cup off the shelf. Then, preheat the oven as the first step, unless the dough is mixed and chilled before shaping. Allow at least 15 minutes for the oven to reach the correct temperature. If you have an oven thermometer, use it to check that your oven is heating to the temperature you have indicated. If it is not, adjust the temperature as needed. For example, if the oven control is set at 350°F and the oven heats only to 325°F, then reset the control to 375°F.

assembling and measuring the ingredients

Get out all of the ingredients you will need for the recipe. The exceptions are those that must be added chilled, such as butter when making crumbly doughs. Measure each ingredient accurately using the proper measuring cups for dry and wet ingredients. Measure flour unsifted, using the sweep-and-level method: dip the appropriate cup or spoon into the flour until heaping, then level off with a straight-edged metal spatula or a table knife blade. Measure dry ingredients in tablespoons and teaspoons by overfilling the standard measuring spoons and leveling the top with the straight edge of a metal spatula or a table knife.

mixing and beating

Most cookie recipes call for a minimum of mixing. A food processor or electric mixer is desirable for bar-cookie crusts and shortbread-style cookies, to create the necessary crumbly consistency. A large spoon is sufficient for mixing many of the doughs, but an electric mixer makes mixing stiff doughs easier, and a stand mixer is indispensable when a whip attachment is indicated. Sifting the dry ingredients for the recipes in this book is not necessary, but it is important to stir them together thoroughly to distribute the leavening and spices evenly before you begin mixing in other ingredients.

rolling out the dough

Use as little flour as possible on the work surface when rolling out cookie dough. Most dough needs to be chilled for at least 1 to 2 hours to firm up before rolling. To speed the process, some doughs may be frozen for 30 to 40 minutes. Many professional pastry chefs roll out the dough between sheets of waxed paper, chill the rolled-out sheets still in the paper, and then peel off the paper and cut out the cookies. If you find this tedious, as I do, skip the waxed paper. Sometimes it is useful to lay a sheet of waxed paper on the dough before you roll it out, especially if it is a soft dough. You can reroll scraps once. Pat them together and chill them again if they have warmed too much. Rerolling them more than once may result in tough cookies.

toasting nuts

For many recipes, the flavor of nuts is enhanced by toasting them in the oven before mixing them into the dough. Place them in a baking pan and bake in a preheated 325°F oven for 8 to 10 minutes, or until light brown (pine nuts need only 6 to 8 minutes). To skin hazelnuts, let the toasted nuts cool for 1 to 2 minutes, then rub the still-warm nuts between the palms of your hands, layers of a kitchen towel, or paper towels, letting the papery skins flake away. It is not necessary to remove every bit of skin.

spacing cookies for baking

Allow ample space between the cookies to allow for spreading during baking. Some cookies, such as Almond Tiles (page 86) and Florentines (page 76), spread more than other cookies. Each recipe specifies the proper spacing.

baking

Allow at least 2 inches of space around each baking sheet in the oven, so that the hot air can circulate freely. In some ovens, you may need to rotate the pan 180 degrees halfway through baking for the cookies to brown evenly. Bake only one sheet of cookies at a time for even browning.

checking for doneness

Check the cookies at least 2 minutes before the time specified for baking them, using the visual cue that is included in each recipe to judge for doneness.

cooling

Cookies should be cooled on the baking sheet until firm enough to be transferred to a rack without breaking. This usually takes just a minute or two. Lace cookies are ideally baked on aluminum foil, as the foil can be slipped off of the baking sheet onto a countertop and the cookies left to cool, at which point the cookies will peel right off. Do not use parchment paper for lace cookies. It prevents them from spreading.

storing

Airtight containers should be used for storing all cookies. It is best to store just one kind of cookie in each container. Frosted cookies should be layered with waxed paper between the layers. Cookies vary in how long they stay fresh at room temperature. Most cookies stay fresh several days at room temperature. Lemon bars are an exception, as they are best within a day or two and should be refrigerated. Frosted cookies and rich chocolate cookies do not keep as long at room temperature as unfrosted, plain cookies. I like to freeze cookies if they are not served within 2 or 3 days, as it better preserves a just-baked flavor. Biscotti and *Springerle* are excellent keepers in an airtight container at room temperature and do not benefit from freezing. If necessary, biscotti gain a fresh-baked flavor with rebaking in a 300°F oven for 10 minutes. Each recipe includes a suggested storing time, but you might consider freezing the cookies after 2 or 3 days as I do. Store at room temperature, unless otherwise indicated.

Most cookies, with the exception of biscotti, freeze well. Put them in heavy-duty freezer bags, expelling as much air as possible, or pack them in airtight containers. Bar cookies can be frozen whole, before cutting. Slip the baked sheet into a freezer bag. As a general rule, cookies may be frozen for 1 to 2 months. They can be thawed at room temperature, unless otherwise indicated.

DECORATING COOKIES

Many cookies are delicious unadorned, but a simple glaze or icing can add a charming and often sophisticated look and a personal artistic touch. The beautiful new decorating sugars in a range of colors and shapes are wonderful for embellishing cutout cookies. Have a selection on hand to add an instant Xmas flair.

Cutout cookies are ideal for icing in a special way. Children and teenagers enjoy giving trees, stars, bells, angels, gingerbread men, and snowmen distinctive personalities. Use the icing to outline the cookies or to add features. The whole family will enjoy giving sugar and spice cutout cookies a holiday profile, a look they only have this season.

A chocolate glaze adds a special touch to biscotti, or it can be used to form a half-moon design on a round cookie, a filling for a sand-wich cookie, or a fanciful drizzle on a cookie of any shape or size. You can dip the end of a cookie bar in chocolate and leave it plain, or immediately dip it into multicolored or silver sprinkles. A shower of powdered sugar—vanilla flavored or plain—gives the simplest cookie a wonderful wintry look.

Another way to decorate your oven output is to turn the cookies into ornaments for the tree, a swag, or a mantel arrangement. Whip up a batch of sturdy cutout cookies such as Gingerbread (page 28), Pepparkakor (page 44), or Mahogany-Iced Brown Bears (page 46), and use a blunt pencil, dowel, or skewer to make a hole in the cookie dough before baking. Alter-natively, stick a $\frac{1}{2}$-inch-long piece of spaghetti into each cookie before it is baked, making the hole at least $\frac{1}{4}$ inch away from the edge of the cookie. Remove the pasta pieces as soon as the cookies are removed from the oven. Slip a pretty ribbon or piece of colorful twine through each hole and hang the ornaments or give away to friends.

PRESENTING COOKIE PLATTERS

In planning cookie platters or plates for a party, consider serving at least four or five kinds of cookies. Offer a variety of contrasting shapes, flavors, colors, and textures. Or for a large party, use a different plate for serving each batch of cookies.

Use your imagination to create eye-catching presentations. Arrange the cookies on an antique silver tray or gold-rimmed platters for an elegant occasion, or stack them in a large Chinese basket threaded with red ribbon and decorated with red and silver glass ornaments for a more casual affair. A beautiful holiday box, outfitted with a big, shiny silk bow and a cluster of silver stars and with its lid to one side, makes a handsome container. Array cookies on plain white platters and surround them with colorful edible flowers, herb wreaths of blue-green rosemary or dense green bay, boughs of holly, or a scattering of dried pine cones. Put together a centerpiece of winter's favorite citrus fruits—oranges, lemons, mandarins, limes, kumquats—and ring it with shortbread and/or biscotti. Or place clear glass platters of cookies atop a sea of deep red rose petals.

A cookie exchange is a great informal way to show off your baking efforts and to discover new cookies at the same time. Contact four or five friends who also love to bake at Christmastime and have them each bake a batch of five dozen cookies. Set the ground rules beforehand, checking on the flavors and types so that the same kind is not duplicated. If five friends each bring five dozen cookies, each person will go home with a dozen each of five different kinds of cookies—and some new holiday recipes.

GIFT WRAPPING COOKIES

Hand delivering cookies to neighbors and friends is a thoughtful custom. Containers can range from a festive paper plate to an antique cookie tin. Other possibilities include fancy clear glass jars, small hatboxes, old-fashioned cigar boxes, pretty bakery boxes, baskets in all sizes and shapes, glass or pottery plates or bowls, or old-fashioned plain round cookie tins dressed up with ribbon and perhaps an ornament for the holiday tree. Also consider new or recycled springform pans, wooden cutting boards, widemouthed glass containers, and, of course, new or even second-hand cookie jars found at a great garage sale or next-to-new shop. It is sometimes nice to tie a cookie cutter and the recipe onto the package.

Utilize colored cellophane for wrapping a festive paper plate. Or pick up a lovely embossed glass plate on a sale table. Gift bags are ideal for sturdy cookies such as biscotti, if you first pack them in a resealable plastic bag. Festoon your cookie gift with satin ribbon, rustic raffia, or metallic twine, and attach a gift tag with a note from your kitchen. Or cut out images from old Christmas cards and paste them on card stock to use for gift tags. Recipes are always welcome, lettered by hand or printed on a card.

BOXING COOKIES FOR MAILING

The best cookies for mailing are nonfragile ones that keep well. Bar cookies are ideal for wrapping in foil and packaging stacked in layers. Fairly sturdy drop cookies can be stacked to form a cylinder and wrapped in plastic wrap. Place the cylinder or layered bar cookies in a gift container, then put the container in a heavy-duty, corrugated box. The box should be larger than the package of cookies to allow room for packing materials, such as bubble wrap, popcorn, newspaper, crumpled paper, or Styrofoam peanuts. It is a good idea to put those fly-away peanuts in plastic bags to tame them, then use the resulting pillows as cushions. Tape the box securely closed, address it clearly, and carry it to your favorite overnight or two-day mailing service.

1

TIMELESS TRADITIONAL COOKIES

2 eggs	Dash of salt
2 cups powdered sugar	All-purpose flour or cornstarch for dusting
1¾ cups all-purpose flour, or as needed	dough
1 teaspoon baking powder	Aniseed for coating baking sheet

 # SPRINGERLE

Makes about 2½ dozen, depending on mold size

THIS CENTURIES-OLD GERMAN COOKIE IS STAMPED WITH A CARVED WOODEN MOLD TO CREATE AN EMBOSSED DESIGN. PLAN AHEAD WHEN MAKING THESE, AS THE DOUGH NEEDS TO DRY OVERNIGHT BEFORE BAKING.

In a bowl, using an electric mixer, preferably fitted with a whisk beater, beat the eggs at high speed until light and fluffy. Add the sugar and continue to beat until completely dissolved and very thick, about 5 minutes using a stand mixer or 10 minutes using a handheld mixer. If using a whisk beater, change to a flat paddle. In another bowl, stir together the 1¾ cups flour, baking powder, and salt. Gradually blend the flour mixture with the egg mixture, adding a few more table-spoons flour if necessary to make a stiff dough. Scrape the dough onto a sheet of plastic wrap and flatten into a disk. Wrap and chill for 1 hour.

Lightly dust baking sheets with flour and then sprinkle with aniseed. On a lightly floured surface, roll out the dough ⅜ inch thick. Dust the surface of the dough with flour or cornstarch and smooth it with your fingertips. Press the mold into the dough, carved side down, and lift straight up. Cut out the cookies using the molded borders as a guide. Place on the prepared baking sheets. Let dry overnight at room temperature; do not cover.

Preheat the oven to 325°F. Bake the cookies for 20 to 25 minutes, or until they turn white on top and pale tan on the bottom. Cool on racks.

Store in an airtight container and let mellow for at least 1 week before serving. They will keep for 2 months.

1 cup unsalted butter, at room
temperature
3 tablespoons powdered sugar
1 egg yolk
$\frac{1}{2}$ teaspoon almond extract
$\frac{1}{8}$ teaspoon salt

2 cups all-purpose flour
$\frac{2}{3}$ cup ground lightly toasted blanched
almonds (page 15)
About 36 whole cloves
Powdered sugar for coating

 # KOURABIEDES   Makes about 3 dozen

SHAPED IN ROUNDS AND HALF-MOONS, THESE GREEK BUTTER-COOKIES ARE AN INTEGRAL PART OF MY FAMILY'S HOLIDAYS. MY MOTHER-IN-LAW ALWAYS BURIED THE WARM COOKIES IN A THICK SNOWFALL OF POWDERED SUGAR. SHE PACKED THEM, TWO OR THREE LAYERS DEEP, IN TINS, AND THEY KEPT FOR A WEEK OR TWO. AT CHRISTMASTIME, IT IS TYPICAL TO IMBED A WHOLE CLOVE IN THE CENTER OF EACH TO SIGNIFY THE SPICES BROUGHT BY THE MAGI TO THE CHRIST CHILD.

Preheat the oven to 325°F. Lightly grease baking sheets, or use nonstick or parchment-lined baking sheets. Alternatively, use nonstick baking sheets.

In a bowl, using an electric mixer or a spoon, cream together the butter, powdered sugar, and egg yolk until light and fluffy. Add the almond extract, salt, flour, and nuts and mix until well blended. Roll the dough into small $\frac{3}{4}$-inch balls or $1\frac{3}{4}$-inch-long crescents with tapered ends, inserting a clove into the center of each one. Place on the prepared baking sheets, spacing them about $1\frac{1}{2}$ inches apart.

One sheet at a time, bake the cookies for 15 to 18 minutes, or until lightly browned. Transfer to racks to cool slightly.

Shake powdered sugar through a sieve onto a sheet of parchment paper or aluminum foil, making a $\frac{3}{8}$-inch-thick coating. Carefully lay the warm cookies atop the sugar and continue dusting them with sugar until they are coated with a layer about $\frac{3}{8}$ inch thick. Let cool completely.

Store in an airtight container for up to 2 weeks.

1 cup raw almonds, or ½ cup each
  raw almonds and skinned, toasted
  hazelnuts (see page 15)
¾ cup sugar
2 eggs
1 cup all-purpose flour
⅓ cup hazelnut flour, almond flour, or
  additional all-purpose flour
1 teaspoon ground cinnamon
¼ teaspoon ground cloves
½ teaspoon ground ginger

¼ teaspoon ground allspice
⅛ teaspoon salt
¼ cup chopped candied orange peel
  (page 77)
2 teaspoons grated lemon zest
⅓ cup sliced almonds (optional)

OPTIONAL ICING:
1 cup powdered sugar
1 tablespoon fresh lemon juice
2 to 3 tablespoons water

 LEBKUCHEN Makes about 1½ dozen

COME WINTER, THE OUTDOOR CHRISTMAS MARKETS IN GERMANY ARE A FAIRYLAND UNDER A DUSTING OF SNOW. IN COLOGNE, MUNICH, AND NUREMBERG, THE CITY SQUARES ARE FILLED WITH LOG HUTS DISPLAYING *LEBKUCHEN* FASHIONED INTO NUTTY ROUNDS OR INTO CUTOUTS IN ALL SIZES OF SAINT NICHOLAS OR OF HEARTS. THE FRAGRANT SWEETS ARE PURCHASED BY THE ARMFUL, AND OFTEN PARENTS SET THEM OUT ON THE NIGHT OF DECEMBER 5, TO AWARD GOOD CHILDREN WHEN THEY AWAKEN THE NEXT DAY, WHICH IS ADVENT. EVERY BAKER HAS A FAVORITE VERSION OF THIS TRADITIONAL RECIPE. THIS ONE IS DELICIOUS— NUTTY, CHEWY, NOT-TOO-SWEET, AND WITH A CITRUS SCENT. THE NAME OF THE COOKIE STEMS FROM THE MEDIEVAL GERMAN *LEBCHEN,* MEANING "HONEYBEE." TODAY IT IS A TERM OF ENDEARMENT.

Using a food processor or blender, combine the nuts and 1 tablespoon of the sugar and grind the nuts finely. Set aside. In a large heatproof bowl, using an electric mixer or a whisk, beat together the eggs and the remaining sugar until light and fluffy. Place the bowl over a pan of gently simmering water, and whisk or beat until the mixture is warm, about 125°F. Remove from the pan and beat until the mixture is thick and light and has cooled to room temperature.

> > >

In another bowl, stir together the flours, ground nuts, cinnamon, cloves, ginger, allspice, salt, orange peel, and lemon zest. Add to the egg mixture, mixing until blended. Cover and chill for 2 to 3 hours, or until firm.

Preheat the oven to 350°F. Lightly grease baking sheets, or use nonstick or parchment-lined baking sheets. Spoon the batter by rounded tablespoonfuls onto the prepared baking sheets, spacing them about 2 inches apart. Sprinkle with the sliced nuts, if not using the icing.

One sheet at a time, bake the cookies for about 15 minutes, or until light brown. Transfer to racks to cool.

If desired, make the icing: In a bowl, beat together the sugar, lemon juice, and enough of the water to make a soft icing. Spread the icing on the cooled cookies. Let the cookies stand until the icing is set.

Store the plain cookies in an airtight container for up to 1 week. Store the iced cookies between sheets of waxed paper in an airtight container for up to 4 or 5 days.

1 vanilla bean

¾ cup plus 2 tablespoons unsalted butter, at room temperature

1 cup firmly packed light brown sugar

⅛ teaspoon salt

¾ teaspoon ground cinnamon

½ teaspoon ground cloves

1 egg yolk

2 tablespoons milk

1 cup ground lightly toasted, skinned hazelnuts (page 15)

1½ cups all-purpose flour

CHOCOLATE GLAZE:

3 ounces bittersweet chocolate

1 ounce unsweetened chocolate

¼ teaspoon vegetable shortening

 # SWISS HAZELNUT HALF-MOONS Makes about 5 dozen

THE SUBTLE SCENT OF CLOVES AND CINNAMON PERMEATES THESE DELICATE GROUND HAZELNUT ROUNDS.

Split the vanilla bean lengthwise and, using the tip of a knife, scrape the seeds into a bowl. Add the butter, brown sugar, salt, cinnamon, and cloves and, using an electric mixer or a spoon, cream together until blended. Mix in the egg yolk and milk. Then add the hazelnuts and flour and mix until blended. On a sheet of plastic wrap, using the wrap, not your fingers, shape half of the dough into a log about 2 inches in diameter. Repeat with the remaining dough. Wrap each log and chill for 1 hour, or until firm.

Preheat the oven to 375°F. Line baking sheets with parchment paper, or use nonstick baking sheets. Slice the logs into rounds ³⁄₁₆ inch thick and place on the prepared baking sheets, spacing them about 1 inch apart. Bake the cookies for 8 to 10 minutes, or until golden brown. Transfer to racks to cool.

To make the glaze, combine the chocolates and shortening in the top pan of a double boiler. Place over hot water and heat until melted, then stir until smooth. Using an icing spatula, spread half of each cookie with the glaze. Chill until set.

Store the cookies between sheets of waxed paper in an airtight container for up to 2 or 3 days or in the refrigerator for up to 1 week.

½ cup unsalted butter, at room
    temperature
½ cup sugar
1 egg
½ cup dark molasses
1 tablespoon cider vinegar
3 cups all-purpose flour
¾ teaspoon baking soda
¼ teaspoon salt
2 teaspoons ground ginger
½ teaspoon ground cinnamon

2 tablespoons unsalted butter, at room
    temperature
2 cups sifted powdered sugar
1 teaspoon vanilla extract
4 to 6 tablespoons water

Red cinnamon candies, green sugar,
    and silver dragées for decorating

GINGERBREAD   Makes about 8 dozen

THIS IS THE PERFECT PLACE TO HAVE FUN WITH THE NEWLY MARKETED DECORATING SUGARS—SPARKLING
ONES, LITTLE BALLS, CONFETTI, AND DECORATIVE DESIGNS. USE THE SUGARS TO DECORATE WREATHS
WITH RED HOLLY BERRIES, TREES WITH ORNAMENTS, SANTAS WITH BUTTONS AND BEARDS, AND BELLS
WITH SILVERY DRAGÉES.

In a bowl, using an electric mixer or a spoon, cream together the butter and sugar
until light. Mix in the egg, molasses, and vinegar, beating until smooth. In another
bowl, stir together the flour, baking soda, salt, ginger, and cinnamon. Add the flour
mixture to the egg mixture and mix just until blended. Scrape the dough onto a
sheet of plastic wrap and flatten into a disk. Wrap and chill for 2 hours, or until
firm.

Preheat the oven to 375°F. Lightly grease baking sheets, or use nonstick or
parchment-lined baking sheets. On a lightly floured surface, roll out the dough
⅛ inch thick. Cut out with 1½- to 2-inch decorative cutters of choice. Or use
larger cutters for gingerbread people. Place on prepared baking sheets, spacing
them about 1 inch apart.

One sheet at a time, bake the cookies for 6 to 8 minutes, or until light brown on the edges. Transfer to racks to cool.

To make the icing, in a bowl, beat together the butter, powdered sugar, and vanilla, then beat in enough of the water to make a spreading consistency. Spread the icing on the cooled cookies, or spoon it into a pastry bag fitted with a fine tip and pipe it decoratively onto the cookies. Immediately decorate with the candies, green sugar, and dragées, then let the cookies stand until the icing is set.

Store the cookies between layers of waxed paper in an airtight container for up to 1 week.

½ cup unsalted butter, at room
temperature
1 cup firmly packed dark brown sugar
3 tablespoons honey
1 egg
2¼ cups all-purpose flour
1 teaspoon baking powder
½ teaspoon baking soda
¼ teaspoon salt
1 teaspoon ground cinnamon

1 teaspoon ground cardamom
½ teaspoon ground allspice
½ teaspoon ground cloves
¼ teaspoon white pepper
½ cup ground raw almonds or skinned,
toasted hazelnuts (page 15)

COGNAC GLAZE:
½ cup powdered sugar
2 teaspoons Cognac

PEPPERNUTS   Makes about 6 dozen

PEPPERNUTS, KNOWN AS *PFEFFERNÜSSE* IN GERMANY, ARE SPICY SWEETS ABOUT THE SIZE OF A HAZEL-
NUT, OFTEN ENLIVENED WITH PEPPER ALONG WITH AN ARRAY OF OTHER SPICES. MENNONITE FAMILIES
ADOPTED THESE COOKIES FROM THE RECIPES OF GERMAN, DUTCH, AND WEST PRUSSIAN BAKERS.

In a large bowl, using an electric mixer or a spoon, cream together the butter
and brown sugar until light. Beat in the honey and egg until well mixed. In another
bowl, stir together the flour, baking powder, baking soda, salt, cinnamon, cardamom, allspice, cloves, white pepper, and nuts. Blend the flour mixture with the
butter mixture. Shape into a ball, wrap in plastic wrap, and chill overnight.

Preheat the oven to 375°F. Lightly grease baking sheets, or use nonstick or
parchment-lined baking sheets. Roll the dough into ¾-inch balls between your
palms and place them on the baking sheets, spacing them about 1 inch apart.

Bake the cookies for 8 to 10 minutes, or until light brown. Transfer to racks.

As soon as the cookies are removed from the oven, make the glaze: In a
bowl, stir together the powdered sugar and Cognac, adding a few drops of water if
necessary. Brush the glaze over the tops of the cookies. Let cool completely.

Store the cookies between layers of waxed paper in an airtight container
for up to 3 weeks.

½ cup unsalted butter, at room temperature
¾ cup sugar
2 eggs
1 teaspoon vanilla extract
2 teaspoons grated orange zest
2¼ cups all-purpose flour

1½ teaspoons baking powder
½ teaspoon ground cloves
¼ teaspoon salt
1 cup dried cranberries or coarsely
  chopped dried cherries
⅔ cup raw pistachio nuts

 CHRISTMAS BISCOTTI   Makes about 4 dozen

BISCOTTI ARE IDEAL HOLIDAY COOKIES, AS THEY CAN BE MADE WEEKS IN ADVANCE AND THEY KEEP BEAU-
TIFULLY WITHOUT FREEZING. IF THEY SHOULD NEED TO BE RECRISPED, REHEAT THEM IN A 300°F OVEN
FOR A FEW MINUTES, AND ONCE AGAIN THEY WILL HAVE A FRESH-BAKED FLAVOR. BY SLICING THE BAKED
LOAVES THINLY, THE COOKIES BECOME BITE-SIZED NIBBLES, WHICH ALLOWS GUESTS TO SAMPLE THE
WHOLE ARRAY OF COOKIES AT YOUR HOLIDAY PARTY.

Preheat the oven to 325°F. Butter and flour a baking sheet.

In a bowl, using an electric mixer or a spoon, cream together the butter and sugar until light and fluffy. Beat in the eggs, vanilla, and orange zest until blended. In another bowl, stir together the flour, baking powder, cloves, and salt. Add the flour mixture to the butter mixture and beat until blended. Stir in the cranberries or cherries and nuts.

Divide the dough in half. One at a time, place the 2 dough portions on the prepared baking sheet and form each into a log about ½ inch high, 1½ inches wide, and 14 inches long. Space the logs at least 2 inches apart.

Bake the logs for 25 to 30 minutes, or until set and light brown. Transfer to a cutting board and let cool for 6 to 8 minutes. Reduce the oven temperature to 300°F. Using a serrated knife, cut the logs on the diagonal into slices ⅜ inch thick. Stand the slices upright on the baking sheet and return the sheet to the oven for 15 minutes to dry the cookies thoroughly. Transfer to racks to cool.

Store the cookies in an airtight container for up to 4 weeks.

PRALINE:

⅓ cup sugar

⅓ cup finely chopped toasted raw almonds (page 15)

¾ cup unsalted butter, at room temperature

½ cup sugar

½ teaspoon vanilla extract

1¼ cups all-purpose flour

½ teaspoon baking powder

1 tablespoon Amaretto or water

 # ALMOND PRALINE WAFERS Makes about 2½ dozen

DUTCH BAKERS LOVE TO INCORPORATE CARAMELIZED SUGAR AND NUT CRYSTALS IN BUTTER COOKIES FOR A WONDERFUL CRUNCHY BITE. THE WORD *COOKIE* IS AN ANGLICIZATION OF THE DUTCH *KOEKJE,* A DIMINUTIVE CAKE THAT WAS TUCKED INTO A CHILD'S STOCKING AT CHRISTMASTIME.

To make the praline, place a heavy 8-inch skillet over medium-high heat. Add the sugar and shake and tilt the pan for 3 to 4 minutes, or until the sugar melts and caramelizes. Add the nuts and shake to coat. Turn out immediately onto a sheet of buttered aluminum foil and let cool. Break into pieces, then whirl in a food processor or blender until coarsely crushed.

Preheat the oven to 325°F. Lightly grease baking sheets, or use nonstick or parchment-lined sheets.

In a bowl, using an electric mixer or a spoon, cream together the butter and sugar until light. Add the vanilla and mix well. In another bowl, stir together the flour and baking powder. Add the flour mixture to the butter mixture along with the Amaretto or water and stir to mix well. Stir in the crushed praline. Drop the dough by rounded spoonfuls onto the prepared baking sheets, spacing them about 2 inches apart.

One sheet at a time, bake the cookies for 12 to 15 minutes, or until lightly browned on the edges. Transfer to racks to cool.

Store the cookies in an airtight container for up to 1 week.

1 tablespoon cardamom seeds
1¼ cups all-purpose flour
⅓ cup granulated sugar
½ cup chilled unsalted butter, cut into pieces
Powdered sugar for dusting

CARDAMOM SHORTBREAD STARS Makes about 22

SHORTBREAD HAS BEEN A TRADITIONAL CHRISTMAS TREAT IN SCOTLAND FOR CENTURIES. THE SPARKLE OF FRESHLY GROUND CARDAMOM, WHICH HAS A ZIPPY LEMON-GINGER OVERTONE, PUNCTUATES THESE SWIFT-TO-MIX COOKIES.

Place the cardamom seeds in a spice grinder and grind finely. In a food processor or electric mixer, combine the flour, granulated sugar, butter, and ground cardamom. Process or mix until the mixture forms fine crumbs. Pat the dough together and knead it on a lightly floured surface until it forms a ball. Wrap in plastic wrap and chill for 30 minutes, or until firm.

Preheat the oven to 350°F. Have ready an ungreased baking sheet. On a lightly floured surface, roll out the dough about ³⁄₁₆ inch thick. With a 2-inch star cutter, cut out the cookies and transfer to a baking sheet, spacing them about 1 inch apart.

Bake the cookies for 12 to 15 minutes, or until the bottoms are golden. Transfer to racks and let cool slightly. While the cookies are still barely warm, dust the tops with powdered sugar shaken through a sieve. Let cool completely.

Store the cookies between sheets of waxed paper in an airtight container for up to 2 weeks.

VARIATION: Omit the cardamom and use in its place ½ teaspoon vanilla seeds, scraped from a vanilla bean split lengthwise.

½ cup unsalted butter, at room temperature
6 tablespoons almond paste
½ cup granulated sugar
1 egg yolk
½ teaspoon vanilla extract
¼ teaspoon almond extract
1½ cups all-purpose flour

MARZIPAN FILLING:
¾ cup almond paste

3 tablespoons unsalted butter, at room temperature
1¼ cups powdered sugar
2 teaspoons light corn syrup
¼ teaspoon almond extract

CHOCOLATE GLAZE:
6 ounces bittersweet chocolate
1 ounce unsweetened chocolate
1 teaspoon vegetable shortening

VIENNESE MARZIPAN BELLS Makes about 3 dozen

A SEAL OF CHOCOLATE COATS THE LAYER OF MARZIPAN THAT LINES THE BOTTOM OF EACH OF THESE COOKIES.
ARRANGE THEM WITH THEIR BOTTOMS UP TO SHOW OFF THE CHOCOLATE TO ADVANTAGE. CONSIDER USING
OTHER CUTTERS IN ADDITION TO THE BELL, SUCH AS A TEARDROP ORNAMENT, STAR, SCALLOPED ROUND, OR
PLAIN ROUND.

In a bowl, using an electric mixer or a spoon, cream together the butter, almond paste, and granulated sugar until light and fluffy, Mix in the egg yolk, vanilla and almond extracts, and flour. Scrape the dough onto a sheet of plastic wrap and flatten into a disk. Wrap and chill for 30 minutes, or until firm.

Preheat the oven to 350°F. Lightly grease baking sheets, or use nonstick or parchment-lined baking sheets. On a lightly floured surface, roll out the dough about $3/16$ inch thick. Using a 2-inch (or other sized) bell cutter, cut out cookies. Place on the prepared sheets, spacing them about 1½ inches apart.

One sheet at a time, bake the cookies for 10 minutes, or until light brown. Transfer to racks to cool.

To make the filling, in a bowl, using a spoon, beat together the almond paste, butter, powdered sugar, corn syrup, and almond extract until well blended.

Using a spatula, spread on the bottoms of the cooled cookies.

To make the glaze, combine the chocolates and shortening in the top pan of a double boiler. Place over hot water in the lower pan and heat until melted, then stir until smooth. Using an icing spatula, spread the glaze over the filling on each cookie. Place the cookies in a single layer on a baking sheet and chill until set.

Store the cookies between sheets of waxed paper in an airtight container in the refrigerator for up to 1 week.

2

FAMILY FAVORITES

SUGAR COOKIES

1 cup plus 2 tablespoons unsalted
   butter, at room temperature
$1\frac{1}{4}$ cups granulated sugar
2 eggs
1 teaspoon vanilla extract
$\frac{1}{4}$ teaspoon almond extract
$3\frac{1}{2}$ cups all-purpose flour
1 teaspoon baking powder
$\frac{1}{4}$ teaspoon salt
Coarse sugar crystals in color of choice
   (optional)

OPTIONAL VANILLA ICING:
2 cups powdered sugar
2 tablespoons hot water
$\frac{3}{4}$ teaspoon light corn syrup
$\frac{1}{2}$ teaspoon vanilla extract
Food coloring of choice (optional)
Red or green sugar crystals for decorating
   (optional)

SUGAR COOKIES
Makes about 7 dozen, depending on cutter size

THIS IS AN EASY-TO-ROLL HOLIDAY FAVORITE TO CUT INTO ANGELS, STARS, BELLS, TREES, OR OTHER DECORATIVE SHAPES. BEFORE BAKING, SPRINKLE WITH SUGAR CRYSTALS, OR BAKE THE COOKIES AND THEN ICE THEM AND ADD A SCATTERING OF SUGAR CRYSTALS FOR TOPPING.

In a bowl, using an electric mixer or a spoon, cream together the butter and granulated sugar until light. Add the eggs and the vanilla and almond extracts and beat until smooth. In another bowl, stir together the flour, baking powder, and salt. Add the flour mixture to the butter mixture, beating until smooth. Scrape out the dough onto a sheet of plastic wrap and flatten into a disk, using the wrap, not your fingers. Wrap and chill for about 1 hour, or until firm.

Preheat the oven to 375°F. Lightly grease baking sheets, or use nonstick or parchment-lined baking sheets.

Divide the dough into 4 equal portions. On a lightly floured surface, roll out one-fourth of the dough about $\frac{1}{8}$ inch thick. Cut into desired shapes using a 2-inch or 3-inch angel or tree cutter. Place on the baking sheets, spacing them about $1\frac{1}{2}$ inches apart. Sprinkle with sugar crystals, if desired, or leave plain and ice after baking.

One sheet at a time, bake the cookies for 6 to 8 minutes, or until light brown on the edges. Transfer to racks to cool.

To make the icing, sift the powdered sugar into a bowl and stir in the hot water, corn syrup, and vanilla until blended and smooth. Add additional hot water if needed to achieve the correct consistency. If desired, tint the icing with a drop or two of food coloring. Spread the icing on the cooled cookies with an icing spatula, or spoon it into a pastry bag fitted with a fine tip and pipe it decoratively onto the cookies. If desired, sprinkle the sugar crystals over the icing. Let the cookies stand until the icing is set.

Store the sugar-topped plain cookies in an airtight container for up to 2 weeks. Store the iced cookies between sheets of waxed paper in an airtight container for up to 4 or 5 days.

        1 cup unsalted butter, at room temperature

¾ cup sugar

        1 egg

        1 teaspoon vanilla extract

        1 teaspoon almond extract

        2 cups plus 2 tablespoons all-purpose flour

Dash of salt

 SPRITZ COOKIES   Makes about 6 dozen

THE BUTTERY SWEDISH *SPRITZ* COOKIE WAS A REGULAR PART OF THE CHRISTMAS BAKING MARATHONS OF MY CHILDHOOD. MY SIBLINGS AND I LOVED CRANKING THE COOKIE PRESS, THEN CUTTING AND TWIRLING THE DOUGH INTO S'S AND O'S. MOTHER OFTEN SHAPED THE DOUGH INTO WREATHS JEWELED WITH HOME-MADE RASPBERRY JELLY. TO SPEED UP THE TASK, USE THE 1-INCH-WIDE RIDGED CUTTER ON THE PRESS TO SQUIRT OUT THE DOUGH IN LONG STRIPS DIRECTLY ONTO THE BAKING SHEET, BAKE THEM UNTIL CRISP, AND THEN CUT THEM ON THE DIAGONAL WHILE STILL HOT FROM THE OVEN.

Preheat the oven to 350°F. Lightly grease baking sheets, or use nonstick or parchment-lined baking sheets. In a bowl, using an electric mixer or a spoon, beat the butter until creamy. Gradually add the sugar and beat until light. Mix in the egg and the vanilla and almond extracts. Add the flour and salt, mixing until smooth.

Pack the dough into a cookie press fitted with a star or ridged tip or any desired design. Press out the dough onto the prepared baking sheets.

One sheet at a time, bake the cookies for 8 to 10 minutes, or until the edges are golden brown. If the 1-inch-wide ridged cutter is used, immediately cut the strips crosswise on the diagonal to make 1½-inch-long cookies. Transfer to racks to cool.

Store the cookies in an airtight container for up to 2 weeks.

½ cup unsalted butter, at room
    temperature
¾ cup sugar
1½ tablespoons light corn syrup
1 egg
½ teaspoon baking soda
¼ teaspoon salt

1 teaspoon ground cinnamon
1 teaspoon ground ginger
½ teaspoon ground allspice
½ teaspoon ground cloves
1½ cups all-purpose flour

PEPPARKAKOR   Makes about 3 dozen

CUTTERS IN THE SHAPE OF PIGS AND GOATS ARE TYPICALLY USED IN FINLAND AND SWEDEN FOR CUTTING OUT THESE VERY THIN, VERY CRISP, PLEASANTLY SPICY SCANDINAVIAN HOLIDAY COOKIES. SOME BAKERS LIKE TO DIP THE HEADS AND HOOVES IN MELTED WHITE CHOCOLATE FOR A TASTY ACCENT. LITTLE PIGLETS ARE FUN FOR CHILDREN TO CUT OUT AND DIP TO MAKE CHOCOLATE SNOUTS.

In a large bowl, using an electric mixer or a spoon, cream together the butter, sugar, corn syrup, egg, baking soda, salt, cinnamon, ginger, allspice, and cloves until smooth. Stir in the flour. Scrape out the dough onto a sheet of plastic wrap and flatten into a disk, using the wrap, not your fingers. Wrap and chill for about 30 minutes, or until firm.

Preheat the oven to 350°F. Lightly grease baking sheets, or use nonstick or parchment-lined baking sheets. On a lightly floured surface, roll out the dough ⅛ inch thick. Using 2½-inch cutters in desired shapes, cut out the cookies and transfer them to the prepared baking sheets, spacing them about 1 inch apart.

One sheet at a time, bake the cookies for 10 minutes, or until light brown. Transfer to racks to cool.

Store the cookies in an airtight container for up to 2 weeks.

1 cup chilled unsalted butter
1¼ cups powdered sugar
2 egg yolks
2 teaspoons grated lemon zest or orange zest
1 tablespoon lemon juice or orange liqueur
2 cups all-purpose flour

1 teaspoon baking soda
1 teaspoon cream of tartar

FRENCH LEMON WAFERS

Makes about 3 dozen

A LOVELY CITRUS SCENT RISES FROM A PLATE OF THESE PRETTY WAFERS. WHEN I MAKE THEM, I USE LEMONS AND ORANGES FROM MY OWN GARDEN, BUT YOU SHOULD ALWAYS CAREFULLY WASH ANY FRUIT, HOMEGROWN OR STORE-BOUGHT, BEFORE ZESTING.

In a food processor or in a bowl, combine the butter and sugar and pulse or mix with an electric mixer until crumbly. Add the egg yolks, citrus zest, and lemon juice or liqueur and process or mix until the mixture comes together. In a bowl, stir together the flour, baking soda, and cream of tartar. Add the flour mixture to the butter mixture and process or mix until blended. Scrape out half of the dough onto a sheet of plastic wrap and, using the wrap, not your fingers, shape into a log about 2 inches in diameter. Repeat with a second sheet of plastic wrap and the remaining dough. Wrap and chill for about 1 hour, or until firm.

Preheat the oven to 350°F. Line baking sheets with parchment paper, or use nonstick baking sheets. Slice the logs into rounds ³⁄₁₆ inch thick. Place on the prepared baking sheets, spacing them about 1½ inches apart.

One sheet at a time, bake the cookies for 8 to 10 minutes, or until golden brown. Transfer to racks to cool.

Store the cookies in an airtight container for up to 1 week.

2 tablespoons unsweetened cocoa powder

3 ounces bittersweet chocolate, coarsely chopped

1½ cups all-purpose flour

¾ teaspoon baking powder

¼ teaspoon salt

½ cup unsalted butter, at room temperature

¾ cup granulated sugar

1 egg

1 teaspoon vanilla extract

1 teaspoon instant coffee powder dissolved in 1 tablespoon hot water

MAHOGANY ICING:

1 cup powdered sugar

1 to 2 tablespoons unsweetened cocoa powder

1 teaspoon light corn syrup

½ teaspoon vanilla extract

2 to 3 teaspoons hot water or coffee

 MAHOGANY-ICED BROWN BEARS Makes 20 to 24

OLDER CHILDREN DELIGHT IN THE PRODUCTION OF THESE CHARMING CHOCOLATE TEDDY BEARS. PRE-TEENS MAY CHOOSE TO MAKE FACES ON THE ICING WITH WHITE CHOCOLATE CHIPS, DRIED CHERRIES, AND GOLDEN RAISINS. THE DOUGH HANDLES WITH EASE WHEN WELL CHILLED AND MAY BE CUT INTO OTHER SHAPES OR INTO ROUNDS FOR ICE CREAM SANDWICHES.

In a food processor, combine the cocoa, chocolate, and ¼ cup of the flour and process until the chocolate is very finely ground. Add the remaining 1¼ cups flour, baking powder, and salt and pulse to blend. In a bowl, using an electric mixer or a spoon, cream together the butter and granulated sugar until light and fluffy. Beat in the egg, vanilla, and coffee and mix until smooth. Gradually beat or stir in the flour mixture, mixing until incorporated. Scrape out the dough onto a sheet of plastic wrap and flatten into a disk, using the wrap, not your fingers. Wrap and chill for about 2 hours, or until firm.

Preheat the oven to 325°F. Lightly grease 2 baking sheets, or use nonstick baking sheets.

Divide the dough into 4 equal pieces. On a lightly floured surface roll out one-fourth of the dough $\frac{1}{8}$ to $\frac{3}{16}$ inch thick. Using a $3\frac{1}{2}$-inch bear cutter, cut out cookies. Place on the prepared baking sheets, spacing them about $1\frac{1}{2}$ inches apart. Repeat with the remaining dough.

One sheet at a time, bake the cookies for 10 to 12 minutes, or until firm. Transfer to racks to cool.

To make the glaze, in a bowl, stir together the powdered sugar, 1 teaspoon cocoa powder, the corn syrup, vanilla, and enough hot water or coffee to make a soft, spreadable icing. Taste and add more cocoa powder for a stronger chocolate flavor, and adjust the consistency with a few more drops hot water or coffee if necessary. Using an icing spatula, spread the icing onto the cooled cookies. Let the cookies stand until the icing is set.

Store the cookies between sheets of waxed paper in an airtight container for up to 4 or 5 days.

1 cup powdered sugar

1 cup unsalted butter, at room
temperature

1 egg yolk

2 teaspoons grated lemon zest

2¼ cups all-purpose flour

⅛ teaspoon salt

GLAZE:

2 cups powdered sugar

2 tablespoons fresh lemon juice

1 tablespoon Framboise or water

 **FROSTY SNOWMEN** Makes about 6 dozen

A SHINY TRANSPARENT GLAZE PERFUMED WITH LEMON JUICE AND RASPBERRY LIQUEUR SHEATHS THESE
TENDER BUTTER COOKIES. HERE, I HAVE MADE SNOWMEN, BUT IT IS FUN TO CUT OUT OTHER DECORATIVE
HOLIDAY SHAPES, SUCH AS STARS, BELLS, BEARS, ANGELS, OR TREES.

In a bowl, using an electric mixer or a spoon, cream together the sugar, butter,
egg yolk, and lemon zest until light. Add the flour and salt and mix quickly to
form a dough. Gather into a ball, wrap in plastic wrap, and chill for 20 minutes,
or until firm.

Preheat the oven to 375°F. Line baking sheets with parchment paper, or use
nonstick baking sheets. On a lightly floured surface, roll out the dough about 3/16
inch thick. Using a 2½-inch snowman cutter, cut out cookies. Place on the
prepared baking sheets, spacing them 2 inches apart.

One sheet at a time, bake the cookies for 8 to 10 minutes, or until golden
brown. Transfer to racks to cool.

To make the glaze, in a bowl, stir together the sugar and lemon juice and
Framboise or water to make a thin, transparent glaze. If necessary, add a few
drops of hot water to achieve the desired consistency. Using an icing spatula,
spread the icing on the cooled cookies. Let the cookies stand until the icing is set.

Store the cookies between sheets of waxed paper in an airtight container for
up to 4 or 5 days.

½ cup unsalted butter, at room
temperature

½ cup granulated sugar

¼ cup firmly packed dark brown sugar

½ teaspoon vanilla extract

1 egg

1 cup plus 2 tablespoons all-purpose
flour

½ teaspoon baking soda

¼ teaspoon salt

1 cup (6 ounces) double or semisweet
chocolate chips or white chocolate chips

⅔ cup dried cherries

¾ cup chopped toasted, skinned hazelnuts (page 15) or chopped walnuts,
pecans, or macadamia nuts

DRIED CHERRY-HAZELNUT CHOCOLATE CHIP COOKIES   Makes about 2½ dozen

DRIED CHERRIES LEND A HOLIDAY SPARKLE AND SWEET-TART FLAVOR TO THE CLASSIC CHOCOLATE CHIP COOKIE, A FAVORITE ON ANY COOKIE TRAY. IT IS EASY TO ADAPT THE RECIPE TO OTHER NUTS, DRIED FRUITS, AND CHOCOLATE, SUCH AS WHITE CHOCOLATE CHIPS AND MACADAMIA NUTS OR GOLDEN RAISINS AND PISTACHIOS.

Preheat the oven to 375°F. Lightly grease baking sheets, or use nonstick baking sheets.

In a large bowl, using an electric mixer or a spoon, cream together the butter and sugars until light. Mix in the vanilla and egg until well blended. In another bowl, stir together the flour, baking soda, and salt. Add the flour mixture to the butter mixture and mix until blended. Stir in the chocolate chips, cherries, and nuts. Using a small scoop, drop mounds of the dough onto the prepared baking sheets, spacing them about 2 inches apart.

One sheet at a time, bake the cookies for 10 to 12 minutes, or until golden brown. Transfer to racks to cool.

Store the cookies in an airtight container for up to 1 week.

½ cup unsalted butter, at room temperature
½ cup granulated sugar
½ cup firmly packed dark brown sugar
1 egg
⅓ cup smooth peanut butter
1 cup all-purpose flour
1 cup quick-cooking (not instant) rolled oats
½ teaspoon baking soda
¼ teaspoon salt

PEANUT BUTTER ICING:
1 cup powdered sugar
½ cup smooth peanut butter
3 to 4 tablespoons heavy cream
12 ounces semisweet chocolate chips or bittersweet chocolate or milk chocolate bars, chopped

❧ SWIRLED PEANUT BUTTER BARS ❧ Makes about 3 dozen

THE CHOCOLATE MELTS TO FORM A DECORATIVE SWIRL WITH THE PEANUT BUTTER TOPPING.

Preheat the oven to 350°F. Lightly grease a 9-by-13-inch baking pan.

In a large bowl, using an electric mixer or a spoon, cream together the butter and sugars until light. Add the egg and peanut butter and mix until blended. In another bowl, stir together the flour, oats, baking soda, and salt. Add the flour mixture to the butter mixture and mix until well blended. Pat into the prepared pan.

Bake for 20 to 25 minutes, or until golden brown.

Meanwhile, make the icing: In a bowl, using a spoon, stir together the sugar, peanut butter, and enough heavy cream to form a mixture that can be drizzled.

When the baked bars are ready, remove from the oven and immediately sprinkle with the chocolate chips or chopped chocolate bars. Let stand for 1 to 2 minutes to melt. Then drizzle the peanut mixture over the melting chocolate and, using an icing spatula, swirl together the chocolate and the topping. Let cool in the pan on a rack. Turn out of the pan and cut into 1½-by-2-inch bars.

Store the bars between sheets of waxed paper in an airtight container for up to 1 week.

6 tablespoons unsalted butter, at room temperature

½ cup granulated sugar

¼ cup firmly packed light brown sugar

1 egg

2 teaspoons grated orange zest

3 tablespoons thawed frozen orange juice concentrate

1⅓ cups all-purpose flour

½ teaspoon baking powder

¼ teaspoon baking soda

½ teaspoon ground cloves

¼ teaspoon salt

1 cup dried cranberries

½ cup coarsely chopped raw pistachios or walnuts

ORANGE ICING:

1½ cups powdered sugar

3 tablespoons unsalted butter, melted

2 tablespoons thawed frozen orange juice concentrate

 # FROSTED CRANBERRY-ORANGE COOKIES

Makes about 3 dozen

TART-SWEET CRANBERRIES LACE THESE SOFT AND CHEWY, ORANGE-FLAVORED COOKIES.

Preheat the oven to 375°F. Lightly grease baking sheets, or use nonstick or parchment-lined baking sheets.

In a large bowl, using an electric mixer or a spoon, cream together the butter and sugars until light. Add the egg, orange zest, and orange juice concentrate and beat until blended. In another bowl, stir together the flour, baking powder, soda, cloves, and salt. Add the flour mixture to the butter mixture and mix until blended. Stir in the cranberries and nuts. Drop the dough by rounded spoonfuls onto the prepared baking sheets.

Bake the cookies for 10 to 12 minutes, or until golden brown. Cool on racks.

To make the icing, in a bowl, stir together the powdered sugar, butter, and orange juice concentrate until smooth. Spread on the cooled cookies.

Store the cookies between sheets of waxed paper in an airtight container for up to 4 or 5 days.

3 COOKIES FOR GIFT GIVING & MAILING

EMBOSSED MACADAMIA STARS

1 cup unsalted butter, at room temperature

$\frac{1}{2}$ cup sugar

1 teaspoon vanilla extract

2 cups all-purpose flour

$\frac{1}{2}$ teaspoon freshly grated nutmeg or ground
   mace

$\frac{1}{8}$ teaspoon salt

$\frac{1}{2}$ cup finely chopped macadamia nuts or
   blanched almonds

Sugar for decorating

EMBOSSED MACADAMIA STARS Makes about 30

AN ANTIQUE GLASS WITH A STAR PATTERN OR A TRADITIONAL COOKIE STAMP CREATES A LOVELY RAISED
PATTERN ON THESE SIMPLE BUTTER COOKIES. WITH THEIR DECORATIVE DESIGN, THE COOKIES LOOK
PRETTY PACKAGED IN A SEE-THROUGH CONTAINER SUCH AS AN OLD-FASHIONED GLASS CANDY JAR OR A
CUT-CRYSTAL PLATE SWATHED IN CLEAR CELLOPHANE. YOU MIGHT TIE ON THE COOKIE STAMP FOR A
SPECIAL GIFT.

Preheat the oven to 325°F. Lightly grease baking sheets, or use nonstick baking
sheets.

In a bowl, using an electric mixer or a spoon, cream together the butter
and sugar until light and fluffy. Mix in the vanilla. In another bowl, stir together
the flour, nutmeg or mace, salt, and nuts. Add the flour mixture to the butter
mixture and mix until blended.

Pour some sugar for decorating into a bowl. Roll the dough into $\frac{3}{4}$-inch balls
between your palms, and place on the prepared baking sheets, spacing them about
2 inches apart. Dip a dampened cookie press or glass rim about $2\frac{1}{4}$ inches
in diameter into the bowl of sugar, then press a ball to flatten, making a circle

with a raised edge. Repeat until all the balls are flattened, dipping the press or glass into the sugar each time.

One sheet at a time, bake the cookies for 15 to 18 minutes, or until golden brown on the edges. Transfer to racks to cool.

Store the cookies in an airtight container for up to 2 weeks.

¾ cup butter, at room temperature

⅓ cup powdered sugar

1 teaspoon vanilla extract

⅛ teaspoon salt

1½ cups all-purpose flour

¾ cup finely chopped pecans or toasted,
   skinned hazelnuts (page 15)

Powdered sugar for dusting

PECAN SNOWDROPS Makes about 3 dozen

THESE RICH, SUGAR-DUSTED COOKIES ARE TIMELESS CLASSICS, POPULAR IN MANY COUNTRIES WHERE
THEY GO BY VARIOUS NAMES, SUCH AS MEXICAN WEDDING CAKES, SOUTHERN PECAN BUTTERBALLS, AND
VIENNESE SUGAR BALLS. FOR GIFT GIVING, SLIP THEM INTO SMALL FOIL CANDY CUPS AND PACK THEM IN
AN ATTRACTIVE TIN OR GIFT BOX.

Preheat the oven to 325°F. Lightly grease baking sheets, or use nonstick or
parchment-lined baking sheets.

In a large bowl, using an electric mixer or a spoon, cream together the butter
and sugar until light and fluffy. Add the vanilla, salt, flour, and nuts and mix
well. Roll the dough into ¾-inch balls between your palms, and place on the
prepared baking sheets, spacing them about 1½ inches apart.

One sheet at a time, bake the cookies for 15 to 18 minutes, or until light
brown. Transfer to racks to cool slightly. Place the still-warm cookies on a sheet
of parchment paper or aluminum foil and heavily dust with powdered sugar
shaken through a sieve. Let cool completely.

Store the cookies in an airtight container for up to 2 weeks.

1 cup toasted, skinned hazelnuts or toasted almonds (page 15)

$\frac{1}{3}$ cup sugar

4 ounces bittersweet chocolate, roughly chopped

$\frac{1}{2}$ cup unsalted butter, at room temperature

1 teaspoon vanilla extract

2 teaspoons Frangelico or Amaretto

2 egg yolks

1 cup all-purpose flour

 # GERMAN CHOCOLATE-HAZELNUT WAFERS

Makes about 3 dozen

SHREDDED BITTERSWEET CHOCOLATE AND TOASTY HAZELNUTS INTERTWINE IN THESE CRISPY COOKIES. STACK THE WAFERS AND THEN WRAP THE CYLINDER IN PRETTY PAPER FOR AN EASY-TO-TOTE GIFT.

In a food processor or blender, combine the nuts and 1 tablespoon of the sugar and grind finely. Transfer to a bowl. Place chocolate in the same appliance and process until finely shredded. Add to the bowl holding the nuts.

In a bowl, using an electric mixer or a spoon, cream together the butter and the remaining sugar until light. Beat in the vanilla, liqueur, and egg yolks until well mixed. Add the flour and the reserved nuts and chocolate and mix until blended. Scrape out onto a sheet of plastic wrap and, using the wrap, not your fingers, shape into a log about $2\frac{1}{4}$ inches in diameter. Wrap and chill for 1 hour, or until firm.

Preheat the oven to 325°F. Lightly grease baking sheets, or use nonstick baking sheets. Slice the log into rounds $\frac{3}{16}$ inch thick. Place on the prepared baking sheets, spacing them about $1\frac{1}{2}$ inches apart.

One sheet at a time, bake the cookies for 10 to 12 minutes, or until light brown on the edges. Transfer to racks to cool.

Store the cookies in an airtight container for up to 10 days.

3 eggs
1 teaspoon vanilla extract
$\frac{1}{4}$ teaspoon almond extract
$2\frac{1}{4}$ cups unbleached or all-purpose flour
$\frac{3}{4}$ cup plus 2 tablespoons sugar
1 teaspoon baking soda
$\frac{1}{2}$ teaspoon salt

2 teaspoons ground cinnamon
$\frac{3}{4}$ cup toasted raw almonds (page 15), chopped into halves or thirds

CHOCOLATE GLAZE:
6 ounces bittersweet chocolate
$\frac{1}{2}$ teaspoon vegetable shortening

CHOCOLATE-SHEATHED ALMOND BISCOTTI
Makes about $4\frac{1}{2}$ dozen

A CHOCOLATE RIBBON GLAZES THESE CRISPY, CINNAMONY BISCOTTI. THEY MAKE SUPERB GIFTS, AS THEY KEEP BEAUTIFULLY IN A HOLIDAY COOKIE TIN OR SLIPPED INTO A PLASTIC BAG AND THEN PACKED IN A FESTIVE PAPER GIFT SACK. I ALWAYS LIKE TO PASS ALONG THE RECIPE, EITHER ON A SEASONAL CARD OR ON A SHEET OF PRETTY PAPER, ROLLED INTO A CYLINDER AND TIED TO THE PACKAGE.

Preheat the oven to 325°F. Grease and flour a baking sheet.

In a small bowl, using a whisk, beat together the eggs and the vanilla and almond extracts until blended. In a large bowl, stir together the flour, sugar, baking soda, salt, and cinnamon. Add the egg mixture to the flour mixture and mix with an electric mixer or a spoon until blended. Stir in the nuts.

Divide the dough in half. One at a time, place the 2 dough portions on the prepared baking sheet and form each into a log about $\frac{1}{2}$ inch high, $1\frac{1}{2}$ inches wide, and 14 inches long. Space the logs at least 2 inches apart.

Bake the logs for 25 minutes, or until set and golden brown. Transfer to a rack and let cool on the baking sheet for 6 to 8 minutes. Reduce the oven temperature to 300°F. Transfer the logs to a cutting board. Using a serrated knife, slice at a 45-degree angle about $\frac{3}{8}$ inch thick. Lay the slices flat on the

> > >

CHOCOLATE-SHEATHED ALMOND BISCOTTI continued

baking sheet and return to the oven for 15 minutes longer, turning them once, to dry slightly. Transfer to racks to cool.

To make the glaze, in the top pan of a double boiler, combine the chocolate and shortening. Place over hot water in the lower pan and heat until melted, then stir until smooth. Using an icing spatula, spread the chocolate over the top surface of the cookies. Let cool until set.

Store the cookies between sheets of waxed paper in an airtight container for up to 1 week.

1 egg
¼ cup honey
¼ cup firmly packed dark brown sugar
¼ cup olive oil, or 2 tablespoons each olive oil and almond or walnut oil
¼ cup thawed frozen orange juice concentrate
2 teaspoons grated orange zest

¼ cup almond, walnut, or whole-wheat flour
2 cups organic or quick-cooking (not instant) rolled oats
¼ teaspoon salt
½ cup golden raisins or chopped dried apricots
¼ cup sliced almonds

 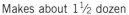

GOLDEN RAISIN-OATMEAL FITNESS BARS

Makes about 1½ dozen

BRIMMING WITH HEALTHFUL GOODNESS, THESE TASTY COOKIES MAKE A DELICIOUS QUICK BREAKFAST OR AN IDEAL SNACK AT ANY HOUR. THEY ALSO MAKE A NEAT CHRISTMAS GIFT FOR THE FITNESS FAN. FRESHLY BAKED, THEY ARE CRISP; AS THEY AGE, THEY BECOME CHEWY. THE DOUGH CAN BE SWIFTLY COMBINED BY HAND BUT NEEDS TO SIT BEFORE BAKING, SO THAT THE OATS BECOME MOIST. SUBSTITUTE CHOPPED DRIED APRICOTS FOR THE RAISINS, IF YOU LIKE, AND ADD ¼ CUP WHEAT BRAN WITH THE FLOUR FOR EXTRA FIBER.

Lightly grease a baking sheet, or use a nonstick baking sheet.

In a medium bowl, whisk the egg until light. Mix in the honey, sugar, oil, orange juice concentrate, and orange zest until blended. Mix in the nut or whole-wheat flour, oats, salt, raisins or apricots, and almonds. Drop the dough by rounded spoonfuls onto the prepared baking sheet, spacing them about ¾ inch apart. Pat down with dampened fingers into bars or rounds. Let stand for 2 hours to soften the oats.

Preheat the oven to 350°F. Bake the cookies for 8 to 10 minutes, or until golden brown. Transfer to racks to cool.

Store the cookies in an airtight container for up to 10 days.

CRUST:

1½ cups all-purpose flour

½ cup firmly packed light brown sugar

½ cup chilled unsalted butter

TOPPING:

6 tablespoons unsalted butter, at room temperature

1 cup firmly packed dark brown sugar

3 tablespoons honey

3 tablespoons heavy cream

2 tablespoons maple syrup

1½ cups chopped pecans or walnuts

½ cup (3 ounces) semisweet chocolate chips

 # CHOCOLATE-PECAN CARAMEL CANDY BARS

Makes about 40

A SWIRLED CHOCOLATE-CARAMEL TOPPING CROWNS THESE HEAVENLY BARS.

Preheat the oven to 350°F. Line a 9-by-13-inch baking pan with aluminum foil and grease the foil.

To make the crust, in a food processor or in a bowl, combine the flour and sugar and pulse briefly or stir to mix. Add the butter and process or mix until crumbly. Transfer to the prepared pan and pat evenly onto the bottom of the pan. Bake for 12 minutes. Transfer the pan to a rack. Leave the oven set at 350°F.

Meanwhile, make the topping: In a saucepan, heat the butter over low heat until it melts and bubbles. Add the brown sugar, honey, cream, and maple syrup and bring to a boil over medium heat, stirring constantly. Let boil without stirring for 1 minute. Pour over the hot crust and sprinkle evenly with the nuts.

Return the pan to the oven and bake for 12 to 15 minutes, or until the caramel layer is bubbly. Remove from the oven and sprinkle with the chocolate chips. Let melt for 1 to 2 minutes, then swirl with a spatula. Let cool. Invert the baked sheet onto a rack, lift off the pan, and peel off the foil. Cut into 1½-by-2-inch bars.

Store the bars between sheets of waxed paper in an airtight container for up to 1 week.

1 cup plus 2 tablespoons unsalted butter, at room temperature

2¾ cups firmly packed light brown sugar

1½ teaspoons vanilla extract

3 eggs

3 cups all-purpose flour

1½ teaspoons baking powder

¾ teaspoon baking soda

½ teaspoon salt

¾ cup whole raw pistachio nuts or chopped pecans

1⅓ cups (8 ounces) butterscotch chips, or 8 ounces bittersweet chocolate or milk chocolate, chopped

 # DOUBLE BUTTERSCOTCH-PISTACHIO BARS

Makes 5 dozen

VARY THESE BLONDIE BARS WITH YOUR FAVORITE NUT-AND-CANDY COMBINATION. PECANS AND CHOCOLATE CHIPS OR PISTACHIOS AND BUTTERSCOTCH CHIPS MAKE WINNING DUOS.

Preheat the oven to 350°F. Lightly grease a 10-by-15-inch baking pan.

In a large bowl, using an electric mixer or a spoon, cream together the butter and sugar until light. Mix in the vanilla and eggs until blended. In another bowl, stir together the flour, baking powder, baking soda, and salt. Add the flour mixture to the butter mixture until well mixed. Stir in the nuts and butterscotch chips or chocolate. Spread evenly in the prepared pan.

Bake for 20 to 25 minutes, or until set and golden brown. Transfer the pan to a rack to cool. Cut into 1½-inch squares.

Store the squares in an airtight container for up to 1 week.

¾ cup unsalted butter, at room temperature

½ cup granulated sugar

½ cup firmly packed light brown sugar

1 egg

¼ cup dark molasses

2 cups all-purpose flour

1½ teaspoons baking soda

½ teaspoon salt

2 teaspoons ground ginger

1 teaspoon ground cinnamon

Raw sugar for coating

❧ SNAP-CRACKLE GINGERSNAPS ❧ Makes about 4 dozen

GERMAN HOUSEWIVES HAVE LONG BEEN MAKING THIS HOLIDAY RECIPE. THE CRACKLY COOKIES CAN BE PACKED IN A REUSABLE WIDEMOUTHED JAR WITH A CLAMP-DOWN LID AND TIED WITH A BRIGHT RIBBON. THEY ARE GOOD KEEPERS.

In a large bowl, using an electric mixer or a spoon, cream together the butter and sugars until light. Add the egg and molasses and mix until smooth. In another bowl, stir together the flour, baking soda, salt, ginger, and cinnamon. Add the flour mixture to the butter mixture and mix until smooth. Cover and chill for 30 minutes, or until firm.

Preheat the oven to 325°F. Lightly grease baking sheets, or use nonstick baking sheets. Pour some raw sugar into a small bowl. Roll the dough into 1-inch balls between your palms, and roll in the raw sugar to coat lightly. Place on the prepared baking sheets, spacing them about 2 inches apart.

One sheet at a time, bake the cookies for 10 minutes, or just until brown on the edges and still barely soft in the center. Transfer to racks to cool completely, or serve slightly warm.

Store the cookies in an airtight container for up to 2 weeks.

4 egg whites

Dash of salt

$^2/_3$ cup sugar

$^1/_2$ teaspoon ground ginger

1 tablespoon grated fresh ginger

$^1/_4$ teaspoon almond extract

1 teaspoon vanilla extract

$1^1/_4$ cups all-purpose flour

$1^1/_4$ cups (7 ounces) macadamia nuts,
almonds, or toasted, skinned hazelnuts
(page 15)

MACADAMIA-GINGER BISCOTTI BATONS

Makes about 4 dozen

THESE CRISPY, WAFER-THIN, NINE-INCH-LONG COOKIES ARE THE AUSSIE'S NOD TO BISCOTTI. I DISCOVERED THEM IN SOUTH AUSTRALIA AT A GARDEN WINE TASTING HOSTED BY THE PRIMO ESTATE WINERY, AND THEY WERE ALSO SERVED WITH HONEY EUCALYPTUS ICE CREAM AT THE RED OCHRE GRILL IN ADELAIDE. THEY LOOK PARTICULARLY DRAMATIC WRAPPED IN CLEAR CELLOPHANE AND GAILY TIED WITH RIBBON, AND THEY ARE AN EXCELLENT SHIPPER.

Preheat the oven to 300°F. Butter and flour a 9-inch square pan.

In a large bowl, using an electric stand mixer fitted with a whip attachment or using a whisk, beat the egg whites and salt until frothy. Gradually add the sugar and beat until stiff peaks form. Mix in the ground and fresh ginger and the almond and vanilla extracts. Fold in the flour and nuts. Spread evenly in the prepared pan.

Bake for 30 minutes, or until set and very faintly brown on the bottom. Remove from the oven, invert onto a rack, lift off the pan, and let cool for 15 minutes. Reduce the oven temperature to 150°F.

Slice the baked sheet as thinly as possible, about $^3/_{16}$ inch thick, making long, slender slices. Lay the slices flat on 2 ungreased baking sheets and return to the oven. Bake for 30 minutes, or until light brown. Turn off the oven and let the cookies dry in the oven for 1 hour longer.

Store the cookies in an airtight container for up to 4 weeks.

1½ cups dried apricots
1½ cups water

CRUST:
⅓ cup firmly packed dark brown sugar
1½ cups all-purpose flour
¾ cup chilled unsalted butter, cut into
   pieces

TOPPING:
3 eggs
1½ cups firmly packed light brown sugar
1 tablespoon Amaretto or rum
½ cup all-purpose flour
1 teaspoon baking powder
¼ teaspoon ground cloves
¼ teaspoon salt
¾ cup chopped walnuts or pecans
Powdered sugar for dusting

 SANTA CLARA APRICOT–WALNUT SQUARES

Makes 4 dozen

THESE CHEWY APRICOT BARS ARE A POPULAR TEATIME AND HOLIDAY PARTY TREAT.

Preheat the oven to 350°F. Grease a 9-by-12-inch baking pan.

Place the apricots and water in a small saucepan. Bring to a simmer, cover, and simmer for 10 minutes, or until softened. Drain, let cool, chop, and set aside.

To make the crust, in a food processor or in a bowl, combine the sugar and flour and pulse briefly or stir to mix. Add the butter and process or mix with an electric mixer until crumbly. Pat into the prepared pan. Bake for 15 minutes.

Meanwhile, make the topping: In an electric mixer, beat the eggs until light in color. Beat in the brown sugar and liqueur or rum. In another bowl, stir together the flour, baking powder, cloves, and salt. Add the flour mixture to the egg mixture and mix well. Stir in the nuts and apricots.

Remove the crust from the oven and spread the topping evenly over the surface. Return to the oven and continue baking for 25 to 30 minutes, or until set. Transfer the pan to a rack to cool. Dust with powdered sugar. Cut into 1½-inch squares.

Store the squares in an airtight container for up to 1 week.

4

ELEGANT PARTY COOKIES

FLORENTINES

1¼ cups sliced almonds

3 tablespoons unsalted butter

3 tablespoons milk

½ cup sugar

3 tablespoons honey

⅓ cup all-purpose flour

⅓ cup finely chopped candied orange peel (following)

CHOCOLATE GLAZE:

5 ounces bittersweet chocolate

½ teaspoon vegetable shortening

FLORENTINES   Makes about 2 dozen

ELEGANT AND SOPHISTICATED, THIS ITALIAN COOKIE GAINS A PROFESSIONAL LOOK WHEN YOU USE FORK TINES TO SWIRL THE CHOCOLATE COATING IN A WAVY PATTERN. WITH A BIG NAVEL ORANGE TREE IN THE GARDEN, I USUALLY MAKE MY OWN CANDIED ORANGE PEEL FOR HOLIDAY BAKING. ONCE MADE, THE PEEL FREEZES NICELY FOR SEVERAL RECIPES.

Preheat the oven to 350°F. Line baking sheets with aluminum foil, then generously grease the foil. Finely chop ½ cup of the almonds. Set aside the remaining sliced almonds for decoration.

In a small saucepan, combine the butter, milk, sugar, and honey. Bring to a boil over medium heat and cook, stirring, for 1 minute. Remove from the heat and whisk in the flour. Stir in the chopped nuts and orange peel. Drop by scant table-spoonfuls onto the prepared baking sheets, spacing them at least 3 inches apart. Sprinkle with the reserved sliced almonds.

One sheet at a time, bake the cookies for 5 to 7 minutes, or until a rich golden brown. Remove from the oven and let cool on the sheets for 1 minute. Then slip the foil along with the cookies onto a countertop and let cool completely. Peel off the cookies from the foil. Place the cookies, smooth side up, on a clean sheet of foil.

To make the chocolate glaze, combine the chocolate and shortening in the top pan of a double boiler. Place over hot water in the lower pan and heat until melted, then stir until smooth. Using an icing spatula, spread some of the warm chocolate on the smooth side of each cookie. Let stand for a few minutes. Using a fork, drizzle the chocolate from the tines, forming wavy lines across the chocolate-coated surface of each cookie. Let the cookies stand until the chocolate is cool. Refrigerate the cookies briefly to speed up setting the chocolate.

Store the cookies between sheets of waxed paper in an airtight container in the refrigerator for up to 1 week. They may also be frozen and thawed in the refrigerator before serving.

---

4 oranges
1⅓ cups sugar
1¼ cups water

CANDIED ORANGE PEEL Makes about 2 cups

Peel the oranges, removing the peel in quarters. Use the fruit for another purpose. Place the peels in a saucepan, add water to cover, and bring to a boil. Drain and discard the water. Again add water to cover, and return to a boil. Drain the water again and repeat one more time. Drain and let the orange peel cool slightly.

With a spoon, scrape off most of the white pith from the peels. In a medium saucepan, bring the sugar and the 1¼ cups water to a boil, stirring until sugar is dissolved. Add the peels and simmer, uncovered, for about 20 minutes, or until the liquid is fully absorbed.

Transfer the candied orange peel to a rack and let stand until dry. Store in an airtight container in the refrigerator for up to 3 weeks, or freeze in a heavy-duty plastic bag for up to 6 months.

2 eggs

6 tablespoons sugar

9 ounces bittersweet chocolate, or
$1\frac{1}{2}$ cups semisweet chocolate chips

2 tablespoons unsalted butter

1 teaspoon vanilla extract

$\frac{1}{2}$ cup all-purpose flour

$\frac{1}{8}$ teaspoon salt

$\frac{1}{2}$ teaspoon baking powder

$1\frac{1}{4}$ cups ($7\frac{1}{2}$ ounces) semisweet chocolate chips

1 cup coarsely chopped toasted, skinned hazelnuts (page 15), walnuts, or pecans or chopped toffee

GIANDUIA SNOWBALLS Makes about 2 dozen

THESE BIG, PLUMP CHOCOLATE BONBONS, WITH THEIR SOFT CENTERS AND CRACKLED SHINY EXTERIORS, MELT IN THE MOUTH. FOR A HOLIDAY PARTY, SHOW OFF THESE GEMS BY STACKING THEM HIGH ON A PEDESTAL PLATE. DO NOT OVERBAKE THEM: THEIR SOFT CENTERS ARE THE SECRET TO THEIR GOODNESS.

In an electric stand mixer fitted with a whip attachment, beat the eggs and sugar until thick and light, about 6 minutes. In the top pan of a double boiler, combine the chocolate or chocolate chips and butter. Place over hot water in the lower pan and heat until melted, then stir until blended. Remove from over the water and let cool completely. Stir the cooled chocolate into the egg mixture. Add the vanilla and mix well. In another bowl, stir together the flour, salt, and baking powder. Add the flour mixture to the egg mixture and mix well. Stir in the chocolate chips and nuts.

Line a baking sheet with parchment paper, or use a nonstick baking sheet. Using a $1\frac{3}{4}$-inch scoop, scoop the dough into rounded balls and drop onto the prepared baking sheet, spacing them about $1\frac{1}{2}$ inches apart. Do not flatten the balls. Place the baking sheet in the freezer for 30 minutes to firm them up.

Preheat the oven to 350°F. Bake for 10 to 12 minutes, or until set but still soft inside. Do not overbake. Transfer to racks to cool.

Store the cookies in an airtight container in the refrigerator for up to 2 or 3 days.

SHORTBREAD CRUST:

    2 cups all-purpose flour
    ½ cup powdered sugar
    1 cup chilled unsalted butter

LEMON TOPPING:

    5 eggs
    2 cups granulated sugar
    6 tablespoons all-purpose flour
    4 teaspoons grated lemon zest
    ¾ cup fresh lemon juice

Powdered sugar for dusting

 # TANGY LEMON SQUARES Makes 4 dozen

A THICK AND ZESTY LEMON LAYER GLAZES A SHORTBREAD CRUST FOR THESE MELT-IN-THE-MOUTH SWEETS, A LOVELY AND TASTY ADDITION TO ANY CHRISTMAS COOKIE PLATTER.

Preheat the oven to 350°F. Have ready an ungreased 9-by-12-inch baking pan.

To make the crust, in a food processor or in a bowl, combine the flour and sugar and pulse briefly or stir to mix. Add the butter and process or mix with an electric mixer until crumbly. Pat into the baking pan. Bake for 12 to 14 minutes, or until a light golden brown. Let cool on a rack for 3 to 4 minutes. Reduce the oven temperature to 325°F.

Meanwhile, make the topping: In a large bowl, using an electric mixer or a whisk, beat the eggs until light in color. In a bowl, stir together the sugar and flour. Add the flour mixture to the eggs and mix until blended. Stir in the lemon zest and juice, mixing until smooth. Pour over the slightly cooled crust.

Return the pan to the oven and continue baking for 25 to 30 minutes, or until just set. Transfer to a rack to cool for a few minutes. While still warm, dust with powdered sugar shaken through a sieve. Let cool completely, then cut into 1½-inch squares.

These are best if served within a day or two. Store in an airtight container in the refrigerator. Do not freeze.

½ cup firmly packed light brown sugar

6 tablespoons unsalted butter

3 tablespoons honey

1 tablespoon heavy cream

¼ teaspoon salt

¼ teaspoon ground cloves

¼ teaspoon ground ginger

½ cup all-purpose flour

¾ cup regular rolled oats

 # NORWEGIAN LACE COOKIES Makes about 4 dozen

THESE SEE-THROUGH COOKIES HAVE A WONDERFUL CHEWY CARAMEL CRUNCH—PERFECT TO ACCOMPANY A PLATTER OF FRESH FRUIT OR HOMEMADE HONEY ICE CREAM. BAKE THEM ON A DRY DAY; OTHERWISE THEY MAY ABSORB MOISTURE AND LOSE THEIR BRITTLE CARAMEL BITE. THE SECRET TO SERENE HANDLING IS TO BAKE THEM ON ALUMINUM FOIL; THEY PEEL OFF EASILY ONCE COOL.

Preheat the oven to 375°F. Line baking sheets with aluminum foil, then generously grease the foil.

In a saucepan, combine the sugar, butter, honey, cream, salt, cloves, and ginger. Heat over medium heat until bubbly. Remove from the heat and stir in the flour and oats. Drop the dough by teaspoonfuls onto the prepared sheets, spacing them about 4 inches apart.

One sheet at a time, bake the cookies for 6 minutes, or until golden brown. Transfer the baking sheets to racks to cool for 1 minute. Then slip the foil along with the cookies onto a countertop and let cool completely. Peel off the cookies from the foil.

Store the cookies in an airtight container for up to 3 or 4 days.

3 ounces unsweetened chocolate

6 tablespoons unsalted butter

1 teaspoon instant coffee or espresso powder

1½ cups granulated sugar

3 eggs

1 teaspoon vanilla extract

1½ cups all-purpose flour

1½ teaspoons baking soda

¼ teaspoon salt

½ cup chopped raw pistachio nuts

2 tablespoons unsweetened cocoa powder

3 tablespoons powdered sugar

About 45 raw pistachio nuts for topping

PISTACHIO CHOCOLATE CRINKLES

Makes about 45

A DUSTING OF COCOA GIVES A DOUBLE-CHOCOLATE BOOST TO THESE CRACKLY-TOPPED COOKIES. EACH IS TOPPED WITH A BRIGHT GREEN PISTACHIO NUT, FOR A FESTIVE CROWN.

In a heatproof bowl, combine the chocolate, butter, and coffee powder. Place over (not touching) hot water in a saucepan and heat until melted, then stir until blended. Remove from over the water and add the granulated sugar, eggs, and vanilla. Using an electric mixer or a spoon, beat until smooth. In another bowl, stir together the flour, baking soda, and salt. Add the flour mixture to the chocolate mixture and mix until blended. Stir in the ½ cup chopped nuts. Cover and chill for 30 minutes, or until firm.

Preheat the oven to 350°F. Lightly grease baking sheets, or use nonstick or parchment-lined baking sheets.

In a small bowl, stir together the cocoa and powdered sugar. Roll the dough into 1-inch balls between your palms, and then roll each ball in the cocoa-sugar mixture. Place on the prepared baking sheets. Top each ball with a pistachio nut.

One sheet at a time, bake the cookies for 8 to 10 minutes, or until firm on the edges but still soft in the center. Transfer to racks to cool.

Store the cookies in an airtight container for up to 4 or 5 days.

½ cup chilled unsalted butter, cut into ½-inch cubes

¾ cup powdered sugar

1 egg, separated

⅛ teaspoon salt

1 cup all-purpose flour

¾ cup finely chopped toasted, skinned hazelnuts (page 15)

Raspberry jam for filling

 # SWEDISH HAZELNUT-RASPBERRY COOKIES

Makes about 3 dozen

A DOLLOP OF BERRY JAM FILLS THE CENTERS OF THESE HAZELNUT-SHOWERED BUTTER COOKIES. ALTHOUGH THEY ARE A BIT TIME-CONSUMING TO MAKE, CHRISTMAS IS THE SEASON FOR SHOWING THEM OFF.

Preheat the oven to 350°F. Lightly grease a baking sheet, or use a nonstick sheet. In a food processor or in a bowl, combine the butter and sugar and process or mix with an electric mixer until crumbly. Add the egg yolk, salt, and flour and mix until the dough comes together.

In a small bowl, whisk the egg white until light and frothy. In another small bowl, place the nuts. Roll the dough into ¾-inch balls between your palms. Dip the balls first into the egg white and then roll in the chopped nuts. Place on the prepared baking sheets, spacing them about 1 inch apart. With the tip of a finger, make a deep depression in the center of each cookie.

Bake for 12 to 15 minutes, or until light brown. Transfer to racks to cool slightly. While still warm, fill each depression with a small amount of jam, then let cool completely.

Store the cookies between sheets of waxed paper in an airtight container for up to 1 week.

3 tablespoons unsalted butter

½ cup sugar

2 egg whites

¼ teaspoon vanilla extract

¼ teaspoon almond extract

¼ cup all-purpose flour

1 cup sliced almonds

 ALMOND TILES Makes about 2 dozen

THIS PAPER-THIN, CRISPY WAFER IS SHAPED AROUND A ROLLING PIN TO FORM ITS TYPICAL CLAY-ROOF-TILE SHAPE. IT IS ONE OF THE MOST POPULAR OF ALL FRENCH COOKIES AND IS OFTEN FEATURED ON THE COOKIE PLATES IN FRANCE'S FINER RESTAURANTS.

Preheat the oven to 400°F. Heavily grease baking sheets.

In a small saucepan, heat the butter over low heat until it begins to melt, them remove from the heat to finish melting. Let cool. In a small bowl, combine the sugar, egg whites, and vanilla and almond extracts. Whisk lightly just to mix. Stir in the flour until smooth. Add the melted butter, whisking until smooth. Stir in ¾ cup of the almonds. Drop the batter onto the prepared baking sheets by teaspoonfuls and spread with the back of the spoon into rounds 3 inches in diameter. The cookies should be spaced 2 inches apart. Sprinkle with the remaining sliced almonds.

One sheet at a time, bake the cookies for 5 to 7 minutes, or until golden brown on the edges. Using a long metal spatula, quickly remove the cookies from the baking sheet and drape them over a rolling pin. Let cool. If the cookies should harden before you remove them from the baking sheet, return the sheet to the oven for 30 seconds to soften them. When the cookies are cool, after 30 to 60 seconds, remove them from the rolling pin.

Store the cookies in an airtight container for up to 1 week.

1 egg

²⁄₃ cup sugar

1 teaspoon vanilla extract

1 tablespoon grated orange zest

2¹⁄₂ cups sweetened shredded coconut

CHEWY COCONUT ORANGE MACAROONS

Makes about 3 dozen

A WHOLE EGG LENDS A PALE GOLDEN COLOR AND RICH FLAVOR TO THESE BILLOWY COCONUT ROUNDS. WITH THEIR SNOWBALL SHAPE, THEY FIT THE HOLIDAY MOTIF.

Preheat the oven to 350°F. Line baking sheets with parchment paper, or use nonstick baking sheets.

In a bowl, using an electric mixer, preferably fitted with a whip attachment, beat the egg until light. Gradually beat in the sugar, vanilla, and orange zest. Continue beating until light and fluffy. Fold in the coconut. Drop the batter by heaping teaspoonfuls onto the prepared baking sheets, making mounds and spacing them about 1¹⁄₂ inches apart.

Bake for 15 minutes. Turn off the heat and let the cookies dry in the oven for 10 minutes longer. The insides of the cookies should still be soft, while the outer surface is crispy. Transfer to racks to cool.

Store the cookies in an airtight container for up to 1 week.

6 ounces bittersweet or semisweet chocolate

1 cup unsalted butter

$1\frac{1}{4}$ cups all-purpose flour

$\frac{2}{3}$ cup unsweetened cocoa powder

$1\frac{1}{2}$ teaspoons baking powder

$\frac{1}{4}$ teaspoon salt

6 eggs

$2\frac{1}{4}$ cups sugar

2 teaspoons vanilla extract

1 cup (6 ounces) white chocolate chips

$1\frac{1}{4}$ cups macadamia nuts, chopped

 ## MACADAMIA-WHITE CHOCOLATE BROWNIES

Makes 5 dozen

FOR A GALA CHRISTMAS PARTY, THIS EXPANDED BROWNIE RECIPE IS IDEAL FOR TURNING OUT A BIG BATCH OF RICH BITES SWIFTLY. SUGAR-SWEET MACADAMIA NUTS AND WHITE CHOCOLATE CHIPS ENHANCE EACH MOUTHFUL. THESE ARE A CROWD-PLEASER FOR ADULTS AND CHILDREN ALIKE.

Preheat the oven to 350°F. Line a 10-by-15-inch pan with aluminum foil, shiny side up, and grease lightly.

In the top pan of a double boiler, combine the chocolate and butter. Place over the lower pan of hot water and heat until melted, then stir until smooth and let cool. In a bowl, stir together the flour, cocoa, baking powder, and salt. In the large bowl of an electric stand mixer fitted with a whip attachment, beat the eggs until light and fluffy. Beat in the sugar and vanilla, mixing well. Stir in the melted chocolate and the flour mixture. Stir in the white chocolate chips and $\frac{3}{4}$ cup of the nuts. Spread in the prepared pan and sprinkle with the remaining nuts.

Bake for 25 to 30 minutes, or just until barely set. Let cool in the pan on a rack, then cut into $1\frac{1}{2}$-inch squares.

Store the brownies in an airtight container for up to 4 days.

VARIATION: For an everyday brownie, omit the macadamia nuts and white chocolate chips and add $1\frac{1}{4}$ cups chopped walnuts or pecans and 1 cup (6 ounces) double or semisweet chocolate chips.

2 cups pecans

⅓ cup powdered sugar

1 vanilla bean, split lengthwise

1 cup unsalted butter, at room temperature

1 teaspoon vanilla extract

1 tablespoon water

1¾ cups all-purpose flour

¼ teaspoon salt

Powdered sugar for dusting

 ## VANILLA PECAN FINGERS Makes about 5 dozen

STACK THESE SNOWY WHITE BARS ON A HOLIDAY COOKIE PLATTER. YOUR GUESTS WON'T BE ABLE TO RESIST THEM.

Preheat the oven to 250°F. Lightly grease baking sheets, or use nonstick baking sheets.

In a blender or food processor, finely grind the nuts with 1 tablespoon of the sugar. Place the remaining sugar in a medium-sized bowl and, using the tip of a sharp knife, scrape the seeds from the vanilla bean into the sugar. Add the butter and, using an electric mixer, cream together until light and fluffy. Stir in the vanilla and water. In another bowl, stir together the flour, ground nuts, and salt. Add the flour mixture to the butter mixture and mix until blended. Spoon out rounded teaspoonfuls of the dough and shape into logs about ¾ inch wide and 1¾ inches long. Place on the prepared baking sheets, spacing them about 1½ inches apart.

Bake for 50 to 60 minutes, or until a very light brown. Transfer to a rack to cool for a few minutes. Dust a sheet of waxed paper with a thin layer of powdered sugar shaken through a sieve, and transfer the warm cookies to it. Sift more sugar over the tops to coat completely.

Store the cookies in an airtight container for up to 2 weeks.

 **SOURCES**

Here are retail stores and mail-order sources for specialty bakeware, specialty sugars, nut flours, nut oils, and other ingredients and tools for the cookie baker. Call for information on mail-order availability.

BROADWAY PANHANDLER
477 BROOME STREET
NEW YORK, NY 10013
TEL: 212-966-3434
Bakeware, specialty ingredients.

CAKE LADY
81A WESTLAKE MALL
DALY CITY, CA 94015
TEL: 650-992-9300
Cookie cutters.

CALIFORNIA PRESS
6200 WASHINGTON STREET
YOUNTVILLE, CA 94599
TEL: 707-944-0343
E-MAIL:
NUTCHIEF@CALIFORNIAPRESS.COM
Almond, hazelnut, walnut, pecan, and pistachio nut flours; nut oils.

DEAN & DELUCA
560 BROADWAY
NEW YORK, NY 10012
TEL: 212-431-1691; OUTSIDE
NEW YORK, 1-800-227-7714
Specialty baking ingredients.

DRAEGER'S SUPERMARKET
1010 UNIVERSITY DRIVE
MENLO PARK, CA 94025
(AND OTHER CA LOCATIONS)
TEL: 650-688-0688
Bakeware, specialty sugars.

GEMSUGAR
4505 SPICEWOOD SPRINGS ROAD
SUITE 306
AUSTIN, TX 78759
TEL: 800-678-8374
Specialty sugars.

GLORIA'S CAKE AND CANDY SUPPLIES
3755 SAWTELL BOULEVARD
WEST LOS ANGELES, CA 90066
TEL: 310-391-4557
Specialty baking ingredients.

INDIA TREE
NO MAIL ORDER OR RETAIL;
CALL FOR PRODUCT LOCATIONS.
TEL: 800-369-4848
E-MAIL: INDIA@NEWLINK.COM
Specialty sugars.

MAID OF SCANDINAVIA
32-44 RALEIGH AVENUE
MINNEAPOLIS, MN 55416
TEL: 800-328-6722
Bakeware.

MAISON GLASS
3180 ROUTE 9
COLD SPRINGS, NY 10516
TEL: 800-822-5564
E-MAIL: MAISONGLASS@AOL.COM
Crystallized sugars, vanilla sugar, pearl sugar, marzipan.

THE NEW YORK BAKING & CANDY SUPPLY STORE
56 WEST 22ND STREET
NEW YORK, NY 10010
TEL: 212-675-2253
Bakeware, specialty ingredients.

PENZEY'S LTD. SPICE HOUSE
BOX 1448
WANKESHA, WI 53187
TEL: 414-574-0277
Spices.

SUGAR & SPICE
2960 JUNIPERO SERRA BOULEVARD
DALY CITY, CA 94014
TEL: 650-994-4911
Cookie cutters and molds, specialty ingredients.

SUR LA TABLE
RETAIL STORES IN WESTERN
UNITED STATES
CUSTOMER SERVICE
TEL: 800-243-0852
Bakeware.

WILLIAMS-SONOMA
RETAIL STORES NATIONWIDE
CUSTOMER SERVICE
TEL: 800-541-1262
Bakeware, specialty ingredients.

 **INDEX**

TABLE OF EQUIVALENTS

The exact equivalents in the following tables have been rounded for convenience.

LIQUID/DRY MEASURES

U.S.	METRIC
¼ teaspoon	1.25 milliliters
½ teaspoon	2.5 milliliters
1 teaspoon	5 milliliters
1 tablespoon (3 teaspoons)	15 milliliters
1 fluid ounce (2 tablespoons)	30 milliliters
¼ cup	60 milliliters
⅓ cup	80 milliliters
½ cup	120 milliliters
1 cup	240 milliliters
1 pint (2 cups)	480 milliliters
1 quart (4 cups, 32 ounces)	960 milliliters
1 gallon (4 quarts)	3.84 liters
1 ounce (by weight)	28 grams
1 pound	454 grams
2.2 pounds	1 kilogram

OVEN TEMPERATURE

FAHRENHEIT	CELSIUS	GAS
250	120	½
275	140	1
300	150	2
325	160	3
350	180	4
375	190	5
400	200	6
425	220	7
450	230	8
475	240	9
500	260	10

LENGTH

U.S.	METRIC
⅛ inch	3 millimeters
¼ inch	6 millimeters
½ inch	12 millimeters
1 inch	2.5 centimeters